Perfectly Placed

Be Where Your Feet Are

Volume 1

May you find encouragement as you read the stories to follow.
XO, Stephanie Meiser

MELANIE WILSON

PERFECTLY PLACED:
Be Where Your Feet Are

Melanie Wilson

Disclaimer
This book contains the ideas and opinions of its author. This book intends to provide information, helpful content, and motivation for readers about the subjects addressed. It is published and sold with the understanding that the author is not engaged to render any psychological, medical, legal, or other personal or professional advice. No warranties or guarantees are expressed or implied by the author's choice to include any content in this volume. The author shall not be liable for any physical, psychological, emotional, financial, or commercial damages, including, but not limited to, special, incidental, consequential, or other damages. The reader is responsible for their own choices, actions, and results.

1st Edition. 1st printing 2024

Cover Concept and Interior Design: Melanie Wilson

Editor: Richard Tardif

Independently Published by
Oxygen Publishing Inc.
Montreal, QC, Canada
www.oxygenpublishing.com

ISBN: 978-1-990093-90-6
Imprint: Independently published

Dedication

This book is dedicated to all women tapping into their radical courage to do the dang thing—whether it be owning a business, keeping your littles alive, loving your husband well, or simply switching the laundry. Life is crazy hard and incredibly messy, but here you are. We all long to be seen in our mess, but recognize that deep within, being truly seen and known is also terrifying. Our radical courage is what keeps us going and keeps us showing up. It allows us to invite others into our mess to be seen, known, and held. God is near to replenish our courage whenever we feel it has been depleted. I am honoring your thoughts, needs, and emotions.

Keep going. *Keep Rising.*

"You are fearfully and wonderfully made"
(Psalms 139: 14)

Table of Contents

v

Foreword

by Tamra Andress

Hey sis, I know you have questions. I know you have big dreams and unmet desires. I know you have weary moments and worries that you keep bringing to the feet of Jesus. We are all more alike than we let on.

We "Martha-around" as the world would have us do, busying ourselves to become all we are "meant to be" or even attempt to build a life that errs on the lens of "successful". All the while, the Mary inside us yearns for rest, peace, and to rid ourselves of all performance. **(Luke 10: 48-32)** To simply be.

I hope by now you've discovered perfectionism is a lie, and pursuing it is detrimental. The only pursuit of perfect that matters is pursuing the perfect one. And he has placed you exactly where you are for exactly this time in history. The enemy wants you to believe otherwise. Stuck in cycles of comparison, competition, unforgiveness, offense, and generational curses; focused on past traumas, limiting beliefs, and big fat lies. Satan is the Father of lies. And this book serves as a coupled weapon, to the Bible, to combat him.

Together, these authors are drawing their swords to sever the ties of the enemy, to loosen the old death clothes **(John 11: 44)** and set the captives free.

This book isn't a tool to pluck yourself out of some current situation, to place yourself on a stage or into a new job, title, neighborhood, tax bracket or marriage... it's meant to help you uncover the expansive blessing that you are in right now, by changing your old mindsets and rewriting the narrative to ignite deep gratitude, unlock fresh wisdom, and propel you into the freedom of this gifted moment.

Here's the truth.

Your placement is your position.

Your position is connected to your purpose.

Your unlocked purpose is your prosperity.

Your pursuit of perfect is your calling.

Now hear me out... don't misconstrue the depth behind these words and take them at surface value, or you'll miss the whole point.

You may have previously been found or perhaps currently find yourself in a place you'd consider hell on earth. You may deem the situation vile, painful, impossible, unfair, disheartening or destructive. And yet, no different than Joseph, who found himself in a pit, enslaved in Potiphar's house or in a prison cell; he ultimately ended up in the palace!

Have you dissected and paralleled this journey from pit to palace for yourself?

Let's go deeper into the details and see if you can extract personal connections and revelations that God himself will use to propel you.

POSITION:

The positions, despite Joseph's placements, were a telltale sign of who God deemed him to be regardless of what man could merely perceive. He was adored above 11 other brothers by his father; he wore the coat of many colors. He was then deemed the head of household for Potiphar; positioned and favored by the prison guards and then placed at Pharaoh's right hand in control of all of Egypt. Ultimately, setting him up for the divine position of caring for the 12 tribes of Israel; his father, brothers and the nations were brought into safekeeping rather than starvation and death. **(Genesis 37-47)** His dream came true, but it took 20 plus years to come to fruition.

How have your past placements positioned you into your today?

PURPOSE:

Perhaps the dream is still to come...

I'd bet you and I are fairly similar to Joseph. You're a dreamer, right? I'm a dreamer too, but that can leave me discontented with my current purpose. Wanting answers now and wanting the vision now. Patience isn't my strong suit.

I can imagine he wrestled with God's plan of action. "Why give me the dream if I can't share it?" "How in the world is that going to happen now that I've been sold into slavery to an entire other group of people?" "My brothers consider me dead... who knows what my Father thinks?" "Why me, God?" Trying to make sense of his brother's actions and each predicament thereafter could have driven him totally insane.

I often think about something that did or will happen rather than being planted and present in my current reality. But I know right NOW I'm still purposed. And when I get present, I now have access to God's presence, and the flow of transcendent peace stills my racing mind and helps me become intentional in my thoughts, words and actions for today... not worrying about what tomorrow will bring, since tomorrow has worries of its own. **(Matthew 6: 34)**

"Discovering purpose" has become a marketing tactic for life coaching and business development, pulling us off kilter to believe we are missing it. But it's always been God's strategy shared biblically and never a hidden secret. Our purpose is to be in a relationship with our Father and to go and make disciples of nations. **(Matthew 28: 19-20)** No one is excluded. It's exactly what Joseph did in EACH position he was in... he shared about God's power in his life through his dreams and dream deciphering, through his integrity and plans of action. He was reliant and in relationship with God, and the where he would disciple and the who he would disciple was revealed through his position.

How are you living on purpose, and who have you been sent to disciple?

PROSPERITY:

Perhaps your immediate fleshly response is premised on resources or lack thereof.

I can't go here without money or disciple them without access... the list of limitations goes on.

As you look at each of Joseph's roles, his positions unveiled and unlocked prosperity time and time again. He had access to more than his wages. And even inside jail, God provided for him through relationships.

Remember: to prosper can also be an activation of the soul. *"Beloved, I pray that you may prosper in all things and be in health, just as your soul prospers."* **(3 John 1: 12 NLT)** To have the revelation and contentment of soul prosperity means your mind, will, and emotions are aligned because of your abiding and therefore bearing much fruit full of favor and bountiful to pass to others **(John 15: 4-5)**. Prosperity didn't look the same in the pit at Potiphar's, in prison, or in the palace. I'm certain Joseph had his fair share of mental battles and convos with God asking "why", but God never left him or forsake him and each situation led him one step closer to his initial dream. Even after his coat was stolen he didn't have to concern himself with what to wear or what to eat, or even where he would rest his head. And while slavery and a prison cell are far from ideal, he was still prospering.

How do I know this?

Because he was walking in righteousness the whole time. His integrity was intact. He was humble and honored those around him, even to those who were in control and far from God. He was still communicating with God to decipher dreams for the inmates. And he never missed an opportunity to explain where his perceived personal power came from. He always glorified God.

Situations and bank accounts may make you feel like you are lacking—but your soul can still prosper because your provider is not man, and provision is a full inheritance, not a partial birthright.

How can you change your mind and come back to the truth of your prosperity that exists right now?

Perhaps it's not money (Joseph had no money), perhaps it's access or bountiful fruit others need that you have (Joseph has leadership and visionary skills). Either way, I can ensure prosperity is the result based on stewardship of what is currently in your hands.

What is currently in your hands to steward?

PERFECT:

None of us will be perfect in this pursuit. Being perfectly placed is God's job and He's the only perfection we will ever achieve.

Society at large is always vying for perfect: the perfect body, the perfect marriage, the perfect job, the perfect house, the perfect kids.

I was surely caught in this vicious cycle since childhood, and it led me to my surrender moment when I finally realized I was living my life in a pit that was perceived to be a platform. It was a facade of perfection that left me empty, alone in a crowded room, and suicidal.

So I pray you take a stand against the tactics of manipulation and don't turn into Joseph's brothers when someone else appears to have something you don't. Nothing of this world, even a fancy coat, will bring fulfillment. And your attention, when not focused on his perfection, will ultimately always lead to emptiness and chaos, (the position prepared by the enemy).

Joseph was eventually wearing a much fancier coat with a much bigger job title, home front, and kiddos included. However, I can ensure, based on his emotional response to bearing witness to his brothers, that he still had a hole in his heart, desiring something we all crave and, regardless of how you present it, is completely intangible: LOVE.

If you set your sights on the perfect One, in time, your position will change, your purpose will be fully realized and you will prosper deep within your soul.

But remember this isn't a tortoise and hare experience called life.

This isn't a handbook composed of rules and regulations of religiosity.

This isn't a rat wheel leading you to burnout.

This isn't an impossible balancing act.

This is a perfectly placed pursuit of the greatest love you've ever known and a life of contentment, coupled with an impact that can very well be the freedom for generations to come.

God has a perfect plan. And you are in a position to prosper.

Let's go!

Introduction

"Why didn't you reach out to me?"

This was my response to a text message from a fellow sister struggling. I often send messages to the women I have gotten to know through many different avenues; to check in and see if I can pray for them or provide support. Usually, the response is a polite "I'm good, but thanks for asking. How about you?"

Oh, the art of deflection.

In the past, if anyone checked in on me like this, my response was usually the same.

Shame!

Shame keeps us silent, bottling up what we need and want to share because we should have it figured out.

Shame!

This was her response to my question. No matter how far you've come, how much wisdom you've gained or the experience you have accumulated, shame can still wield power over you. It is quiet and sneaky and creeps in without us knowing its presence. It reminds me of carbon monoxide, a deadly gas without taste or smell. Its victims are usually oblivious unless an alarm alerts them to it. Much like shame, it may be impossible to detect.

This is a rhetorical question, but are you familiar with the Bible? At some point, many have encountered it. Maybe it was a gift as a child, found in the top drawer in a hotel room, on the back of a pew, or handed to you in some form as you walked the streets of a busy city; you are somewhat familiar with the Bible. However, for many, it's just a book. It has no meaning or significance in their lives. Words on pages. Ink on paper. Inside the cover, marked: Bible.

However, inside is where you learn to be equipped to declare victory over shame as often as you need to. The wisdom on these pages is like the alarm that can alert you when something harmful is approaching sneakily and unexpectedly. Harnessing the power from within the Bible is not an easy pursuit. It is not an easy read, and even more cumbersome to see how it is relevant or applicable to our lives.

But, when the words on those pages come to life, and you get to experience the promises, you hold on tight to the hope and stand a little taller. Fortunately, my fellow sister and I have a deeply rooted friendship built on our faith in Jesus. Because of this, there is a sense of safety, and being vulnerable and honest is encouraged and non-negotiable. She knows my story, and I know hers. As a result, there is trust and confidence in communicating the truth so that shame can be destroyed. She responded honestly to my question, which gave us the proper support and encouragement.

Sharing our stories is necessary because it evokes emotion, vulnerability, and authenticity. Compassion comes from understanding the truth and how to love without judgment and courageously supporting each other. It conveys an unspoken permission that it is also okay to share your story.

As these stories are told, shame recedes.

Shame is a form of darkness; the light takes over when we speak about our struggles and pain. They can no longer exist or cripple us.

Resilience emerges as a central theme throughout this collection of personal accounts, which are true testimonies of the power of God. Because of Him, these women can share what they endured and how they overcame, or may still be in the process of overcoming. In these narratives you see the words written on the pages of the Bible come to life. It becomes real, relevant, and relatable. You may see yourself in one or more of these stories captured in this book's chapters, which may become the pivotal moment in your life that sets in motion things you once thought were impossible.

At some point, these women had to embrace that they were perfectly placed and simply be where their feet are to allow God to move and transform them. Their stories are about glory, triumph, and victory. Much like the stories in the Bible, we see warriors fighting battles and our God showing up in ways only He can, to provide forgiveness, freedom, and salvation.

You may not see it now, but you are also perfectly placed. Be where your feet are and witness what He can do with your obedience. You do not need to have all the answers, because God is still in control. God is still holding your heart.

"But forget all that–It is nothing compared to what I am going to do. For I am about to do something new. See, I have already begun! Do you not see it? I will make a pathway through the wilderness. I will create rivers in the dry wasteland."

(Isaiah 43: 18-19 NLT)

Chapter 1

Finding my place

by Lacey Huff

She's a lover of life with a mischievous twinkle, fiercely tenacious, fearless, empathetic, and a champion for everyone, including herself. But this darling girl, through many painful experiences, lost much of her God-given identity over the years. Some of those experiences created an environment where she tended to hide, to seem small and non-threatening.

I knew this girl, and the only explanation I can imagine that would have made her become less of herself, who God called her to be, is that she must have thought it was the most loving and protective thing she could do. However, the core of her God-given identity had remained intact, and by His grace, this girl is making a comeback!

Friend, do you see yourself in this girl? If so, accompany me, and I'll tell you her story.

Rewind seven years—the volcano erupts

He had to tell me that he got fired. FIRED! F.I.R.E.D. Not JUST fired... fired for what? Initially, I was numb. I went into fact-finding and fix-it mode. I made calls. How could he? Why didn't someone tell me? My mind flashed back to the last few months of intense arguments, years of issues, and things that didn't line up or make sense.

My suspicions had been correct. Why didn't I trust my gut? I knew, but I doubted myself. Betrayal stings. It shreds. It rips the heart and soul out of a human and turns the mind into a place that isn't home anymore. Trust, confidence, and everything you think you know or have convinced yourself to believe vanishes, nowhere to be found.

Why now? I thought we had finally made it. After 12 challenging years, we overcame obstacles, achieved financial stability, fostered a strong community of friends, and, alongside our children, successfully constructed the home of our dreams by hand. This town had become our cherished home. However, the reality differed from my bold proclamation and belief that we were entering a thriving season!

But. We. Were. Not.

What looked like thriving was a fragile facade housing miserable lies and only one of us was privy to the details; it wasn't me.

I believed it would break us so awfully, but once healed, we would resurrect like that phoenix rising out of the ashes. I had a renewed sense of hope. We would grow and love and be healthy and whole, finally! Of course, it took me weeks, if not months, to come to that hope. And so we danced the dance. Two steps forward, three steps back, until we settled into a sense of normalcy.

I was fighting, working, praying, and pulling up my bootstraps repeatedly, but to no avail. I feared there would be no mom left in me for my kids. A woman couldn't carry her family on her back for long without it breaking her, maybe killing her. We were not meant to do this alone. It should be two people working together. Two people committed to loyalty and faithfulness. Two people dedicated to growing together in vulnerability and emotional connection.

The beautiful truth

The truth will set you free. There was a shift that took place. My mind began to be renewed by the power of the Holy Spirit. I started believing actions over words that told me everything I needed to know. I saw my value like I never had before. So, I quit my part-time job and began a business to allow me the flexibility to spend more time with my kids. That quickly grew into me working a lot more instead and, in the back of my mind, wondering if I could make enough money to support myself if I did move forward with a divorce.

Then I got a sign.

My beautiful grannie fell on her deathbed. I quickly planned a trip to see her. God was about to move powerfully, and he would reveal His future for me.

"There is no reason to be married for 65 years just to say you've been married for 65 years," she said.

Wow! But what about "marriage is forever?" Is it? Is it God's design that you be bound to a marriage where you have been betrayed? Is that the place He has for His beloved daughter? Why was Grannie only now sharing this—baring her soul to me? Maybe she didn't have a support system? Perhaps she feared being alone? Maybe she just couldn't, but God knew I could.

He heard my prayers and cries. He answered them in a way only He could. My Grannie may not have had the means to get out of her situation, but she did have the determination and grit that she passed along, and by the grace of God, I was going to rediscover it.

On our 21st anniversary, ten days after what I now refer to as, "the straw that broke the camel's back" (this momma's back), I told my husband that I would not be "sticking this out," and then all hell broke loose...

The aftermath

I stepped out of the Church and into the parking lot. The familiar place that I had walked in and out of with my family of five for the last ten years. The place where I took part in youth nights and car washes, where I greeted people as they walked through the door on Sunday mornings. The place I walked in and out of for leadership meetings, and as a volunteer for children's church, where I toted baked goods, paint brushes, rakes and shovels, depending on what was needed, but this time the air felt unbreathable.

Did she fall from faith? Did she cheat? Poor kids. Does she even go to church anymore? Marriage is forever. The grass isn't always greener. They were the perfect couple. She's one of those people who needs to "find herself." The weight of these words draped the "scarlet letter" around my neck. It wasn't an "A." It was a "D."

If you have the unfortunate disposition, as I do, that causes you to subject yourself to be concerned about the opinion of others, you know it's a terrible position to be in, to be labeled the leaver. It is a brutal injustice. Do I have the plague? Is this contagious? I lost friends I thought were forever. I lost the community that I left my blood, sweat, and tears alongside. Shunned. I didn't fit in where I used to.

My feet felt unmovable. The emotional pain hit like shrapnel. I wanted to die.

"Take me out of here, God. How could this be? What is even happening?"

I bared my heart concerning my marriage; I finally told someone all the things from all the years, and suddenly I was labeled as "delusional" with the letter "D" draped around my neck.

The words raced through my mind. For months, those words would continue to hold me, their unsuspecting victim, a prisoner, sending my soul into a whirlwind of despair from which I thought I would never be free.

"You're outside the will of your heavenly Father."

"You're running away from suffering."

"You are called to be part of the solution for your one-flesh partner."

"You are disobedient if you follow through with the divorce."

"You're allowing your fear and wounds to guide you."

"If you leave, a hell is coming; it's just a different kind of hell than the one you're already in."

"God hates divorce."

I cannot understand. I will never understand. The agenda that took over my life for months included flipping the script so that I was no longer the victim but now the offender. The truth wasn't enough for "them." I had hoped to be wrapped in a comforting blanket of compassion, empathy, and a helping hand. Instead, I was greeted with a blanket of torment, doused in gasoline, more fuel to add to the fire of my self-doubt, and a harsh hand to strike a match, no, a box of matches, that would be sure to quiet me and put me in my place.

Over several months, I was bullied and harassed instead of receiving love and support. Be in the "community," but don't dare say what you are going through. Be "authentic," but no mess is allowed as long as the outside of the cup is clean, to hell with the inside.

Normalize. Minimalize. Shh. Shhh. SHHHH!

If it weren't for friends and my family, I believe it would have killed me. Imagine drowning, but then you somehow grabbed hold of that lifesaver, only to have it ripped from your grip by the ones who you thought were there to save you. Then, once they snatch it from your outstretched hands, they push you under the surface until you're sure to take that last breath of water into your lungs. They then leave you to sink to the ocean floor, never to be recovered.

That was me until I decided to rise and speak up.

This is who we are! A She'll Rise Woman.

Now, I can breathe. I can feel. I have found a home, and it lives inside of me. I live and laugh. I have found a love that heals and doesn't wound. I am not afraid of what's in front of me. I embrace life with open arms because I know that I am in the faithful hands of a good God, who sees me, hears me, and loves me. I found my voice. I am finding my place. And I am reaching out to the next woman and the next one who needs help to know who and whose she is.

Our God-given identity

The stripping away of our God-given identity will do us in and render us ineffective in the Kingdom of God; allowing self-doubt to linger, neglecting to use your God-given voice, and choosing to believe a lie rather than the truth can erode our God-given identity. It can be subtle and slow.

You can hear the Holy Spirit. You have direct access to your Creator. You can decipher His written words. You are allowed to be who God has called you to be. You are allowed to ignore the voices that tell you otherwise. You can expect to be loved and emotionally safe in a marriage. You are allowed not to want to be manipulated, bullied, or lied to. You are allowed dignity and respect.

You have permission to figure out who you are after enduring trauma and betrayal, whether it was one time or years of more things than you can count. You are allowed not to know what to do. You are allowed to take up beautiful space on this earth. You're allowed to change.

Discover your strength, resilience, and the power of reclaiming your true identity. My darling friend, if you've ever felt the weight of labels, betrayal, and self-doubt, break free from societal expectations and embrace your God-given right to be who you are. You aren't a leaver or a quitter labeled with a scarlet "D." You're a vibrant soul, tenacious, empathetic and a champion. Past hurts may have dimmed your light, so reclaim it. You're no quitter. You're brave, valuable, and worthy of a voice. God will never abandon you. He will place you perfectly.

Find solidarity in the journey of rising above challenges. Rise with us—be a She'll Rise Woman!

Lacey has been a devoted follower of Jesus since she was very young and believes nothing is worth pursuing if God isn't at the center. She is a licensed Realtor and a full-time student pursuing a psychology degree.

The joy of her life has been raising her three boys, who are now adult men. Lacey is a Florida native who recently moved back to her hometown of Fort Myers and will soon marry a man God graciously brought into her life at the right time. Through that, she has been blessed with three awesome bonus kids.

Chapter 2

When You Experience God Winks

by Dr. Robyn Graham

It was September 2005.

The package I'd been waiting for finally arrived. I opened it with joyful anticipation that I'd find the home décor piece I'd ordered. I had eagerly awaited its contents to complete the family room decorating project. I had long since forgotten about that item, but the God Wink surprise waiting in the box was all that mattered.

After removing the layers of gray packing paper, I read the words from **Jeremiah 29: 11**, "*For I know the plans I have for you, declares the Lord, plans to prosper you and not to harm you, plans to give you hope and a future.*"

Tears filled my eyes and steadily streamed down my cheeks. I covered my mouth the way one does when in shock. The item came when I was experiencing the most difficult challenge of my life. My daddy, whom I loved deeply and depended on, was battling stage 4 esophageal cancer. We had little earthly hope.

Our hope rested in our faith and the miraculous power of our merciful and mighty God. Daddy would say, "Don't cry for me. I'm in a win-win situation. If I survive, I get a miracle of healing on earth. If I don't, I get miraculous healing in heaven." But my heart could only expect the pain of not having him here with me.

There were many days, sometimes multiple times, when I would ask God, "Why? I wasn't ready for this. My daddy, the epitome of health, was supposed to be at all my boys' games, graduations, and weddings. I still needed him; I was his little girl. The thought of not having him was more than my sensitive heart could fathom.

But every time I questioned, I heard, "For I know the plans I have for you..."

Facing death and loss is traumatic and frightening. It's the pain that drops you to your knees, only to form a puddle of emotional turmoil on the floor.

But what I learned from God and Daddy through this experience changed my life. I was never alone. And God had a purpose for me.

My God Wink gave me hope for the future. And God's plan appeared when friends began losing loved ones. I could hold and support them in an impossible way had I not gone through the trial myself.

Seeing learned a life lesson of faith, trust, and hope.

My "whys" weren't only directed at God. I'd ask my daddy to shed wisdom and light on the dreadful situation. And do you know what he told me?

Just as he wore a tool belt for work, God was using him as a tool to witness Christ's grace and mercy. He elaborated that if he could bring one person to faith and baptism, he would have served his purpose. And he did. Shortly after Daddy passed away, his young neighbor underwent baptism.

Friend, God is winking at you today. He has created a great plan for you. You are His, and He has hope and a future for you. And He will equip you for all He has planned for you. As you seek answers and tools you need, you will find them. Knock and doors will be open to you. **(Matthew 7: 7- 8)**

Never discount experiences. Be grateful to each one because you will learn and grow and be blessed powerfully on the other side. Listen attentively to conversations. Look for little miracles and blessings; they are all around you because God has surrounded you with His love and grace. He lives in you with the Holy Spirit, who guides you. And when God Winks, give gratitude for the unexpected and granted smile. I've experienced more God Winks than I could ever imagine.

And I know you will, too.

Seeing God Winks

Inspired by **Philippians 4: 6-7**, "*Do not be anxious about anything, but in every situation, by prayer and petition, with thanksgiving, present your requests to God. And the peace of God, which transcends all understanding, will guard your hearts and your minds in Christ Jesus,*" I made the decision that I was going to pray for my kids and turn them over to God each morning because I didn't want the worry and anxiety to overwhelm me throughout the day. And I knew He had a much more positive influence over them than my worry could ever have.

That trust paid off. I would never have survived the debilitating anxiety and worry over what could happen when my children left my nest. Deep down, I knew it was also best to let them live and have experiences to learn from rather than being a worrywart helicopter parent.

One chilly, damp fall morning, when my son was driving to school, he lost control of his car. I was home with my daughter when the phone rang. It was my son, Samuel. I immediately packed up my daughter, and we drove as fast as possible to the scene of the accident. Fortunately, my son was not alone. The friend and teammate he drove to school each day was with him. His friend's father was in the area and arrived shortly after the accident.

My first sight on the scene was the slate gray Acura MDX mangled. Emotions flooded me. Then, I saw my son standing on the opposite side of the road with his friend and his friend's father. I ran to him. I hugged him—and made sure he was okay. Miraculously, he was. I do not know how, other than God was watching over him.

The car was wrecked.

His friend's father drove them to school, where they checked in with the nurse, and she observed them for the day. Both were injury-free.

When my daughter and I drove home, we came to a T intersection with an open field in front of us. Sitting straight ahead and peering at us was a bald eagle. Tears flooded my eyes, and gratitude overwhelmed my heart as I knew immediately, without question, God was delivering a message—a God wink—that He had protected Samuel, and I could always trust Him.

I'm not saying bad things don't happen; they do. But when we surrender to Jesus, we will see His hand (and eyes) in everything we experience. We can't control the enemy or the world around us, but we can choose to put our faith, trust, and hope in God.

The Bible refers to eagles many times. It often represents God's loving care for His people. A favorite verse that provides a lot of peace and reflects my God wink is **Isaiah 40: 31**, which reads, "*But those who hope in the Lord will renew their strength. They will soar on wings like eagles; they will run and not grow weary; they will walk and not be faint.*"

Hearing God Winks

Prayer gives us hope. Have you ever prayed about something and felt overwhelmed with all the decisions you could make? But then, you are in conversation with a friend, and she says something and bingo, you have your answer. I call those God Winks. God is speaking directly to you through someone else when you are about to give up on prayer and least expect Him to answer.

Pay attention when navigating a situation, relationship, trial, or facing a decision. Get curious. Listen. Observe. God speaks to us in so many ways.

Psalm 37: 4 encourages us to pray. "*Delight yourself in the Lord, and He will give you the desires of your heart.*" He always hears you. He always answers you. But you are responsible for hearing Him and discerning what you hear.

And if you need a reminder, like I often do, reflect on **Deuteronomy 31: 8**, "*It is the Lord who goes before you. He will be with you. He will not leave you or forsake you. Do not fear or be dismayed.*"

He knows your needs, sweet friend. And we have unending hope in Him. **Lamentations 3: 21-23** reminds us of this hope. "*Yet this I call to mind and therefore I have hope: Because of the Lord's great love we are not consumed, for his compassion never fails, they are new every morning; great is your faithfulness.*"

Have faith. In it lies hope.

The surprise of God Winks

Sometimes, a God Wink comes in physical form. After my father passed away, my sons were both in school full days. Even though I was working when I was home alone, I was lonely. After all, I'd gone from talking to Daddy on the phone several times a day and having at least one son home half a day, to quiet and stillness for six to eight hours at a time.

One afternoon, when on the phone with my husband, I said, "I'm lonely. Maybe we should get a puppy."

The next thing we knew, I was pregnant on our 10th wedding anniversary. As two pharmacists with a surprise pregnancy, we received a lot of questions.

Daddy always said, "You don't need a third child, you have two beautiful, healthy boys, man-to-man defense, and you don't want a middle child." (He was a middle child).

But God knew better, or maybe Daddy collaborated with Him when he arrived in Heaven, reminding God that I needed a daughter to care for me someday.

That little surprise has been the best blessing ever. I didn't know it then, but I needed a daughter to complete our family and to fill my heart with the missing piece of the puzzle.

She is a God wink in human form.

He will wink at you.

Friend, never doubt that God is communicating with you.

Trust. Discern.

And watch and smile as He winks at you.

Dr. Robyn Graham is the founder and owner of Robyn Graham, LLC, and the creator of the Purpose to Results™ - Success without Social Method. With an emphasis on mindset, strategy, and action for one-stop business growth coaching, she helps small business owners grow sustainable businesses for a lifetime of limitless earning potential while having a meaningful impact without focusing on social media.

Robyn is a business growth strategist and coach, host of the globally acclaimed podcast The Robyn Graham Show, a speaker, and the best-selling author of You, Me, and Anxiety: Take Action Over Anxiety to Enjoy Being You, in which she shares her life-long journey with anxiety to help others navigate their anxiety to live a joyful, peaceful, purposeful life.

When not working, you'll find Robyn spending time with her husband, three children, and two dogs, most likely doing an outdoor activity, traveling, or enjoying great food. She is also on the board of directors for Face to Face Germantown.

Chapter 3

Change the Narrative

by Rachel Toa

Throughout my life, I've assumed the role of the "strong" one, shouldering the overwhelming burden of the world and believing I was solely responsible for everyone's happiness. This sentiment intensified, as it seemed like the world was conspiring against me. Growing up in a divorced household further contributed to my perspective. My mother's journey, marked by multiple back surgeries and illnesses, relocations to unfamiliar towns, and the challenges of navigating womanhood, collectively shaped the trajectory of my life.

While these challenges have undeniably influenced the person I've become, not every chapter has yielded positive outcomes. Throughout the years, I've confronted depression, wrestled with suicidal thoughts, faced addiction, and presently, debilitating anxiety.

My joy is tied to the welfare of those in my vicinity, a sentiment I think resonates with many women. This inclination has substantially shaped my career path as a pediatric hematologist and oncology nurse, aligning with a lifelong dream.

However, while this career allows me to fulfill a calling inspired by Jesus, it comes with challenges. One notable example is the need to maintain a brave face for my patients during their most difficult moments, concealing personal struggles to ensure they receive the best care.

Now in my mid-30s, I am navigating life as a divorcee and the mother of a beautiful little girl. I still carry the world's weight on my shoulders; both my mind and body have reached a breaking point. I feel like a robot on the verge of screaming, crying, and curling up in a fetal position. Daily struggles with panic attacks, crying spells, and anger outbursts have become hauntingly familiar. Deep down, I sensed that something had to change. I knew it was time to address the turmoil within.

Observing my daughter peacefully asleep beside me one night, I realized she deserves a better version of her mother than I have become. At that moment, lying in bed, panic overwhelmed me. Fear seized my entire body, inducing a chilling sensation, muscle tremors, pounding in my ears and chest, and rapid breaths. Gradually, I grounded myself, recognizing this episode as another panic attack, tears streaming down my face. In desperation, I cried out to Jesus, confessing, "Father, I'm sorry. I've been trying to handle everything on my own. Please help me."

Lying there, careful not to disturb my daughter, the trembling gradually eased, the tears slowed, and my breathing returned to a slower, more restorative pace. At that moment, I encountered the Lord's presence in a previously unknown way. A profound sense of peace enveloped me, satisfying a deep yearning within my body. Changes were imperative for healing.

Growing up, I always knew Jesus. I participated in youth groups, accepted Him as my Lord and Savior at 20, and led youth in my church for four years. It's remarkable how I was consistently willing to help others find Jesus, yet I often felt like He was too busy for me.

I hesitated to burden Jesus with my problems, convincing myself that others needed Him more than I did. However, Jesus reminds me subtly and sweetly, "If you only knew how much I love you." Whether through the thoughtful actions of a friend, paying attention to moments of glory in my life, or truly listening to His voice, these reminders have been a source of comfort.

Many physicians recommended medication to ease my panic attacks, but making that decision proved challenging for me. Despite consulting various medical professionals for guidance, I found myself in a persistent struggle.

Turning to the ultimate healer and provider, Jesus, I sought clarity. I prayed, requesting a clear sign regarding whether I should take the medication. I was adamant about not proceeding unless He offered a clear directive. In a lighthearted moment, I even expressed, "I need a sign like a brick on the head or something here, Jesus." I sensed a connection instantly, as if He understood my desperation, perhaps even chuckling at my candid plea.

Then, I heard the most calm, stern, and loving voice. "I am your medicine." Clarity struck, and I comprehended the steps

I needed to take. I reshaped my daily schedule, giving priority to Jesus. Each morning begins with prayer and quiet time, and I continue to pray throughout the day. Deliberately, I speak positive affirmations over myself, allocating time to journaling and reading His word.

I acknowledged the necessity of eliminating the addictions that were filling the void rather than relying on Jesus. Daily drinking, initially a means of relaxation, proved more harmful than beneficial. I was chugging caffeine like it was water because of sleep deprivation, exacerbating my anxiety.

While I'd love to declare that my entire existence has been transformed and I'm floating on a cloud of sunshine, the truth is different. Each day continues to be a conscious decision and an ongoing struggle. I grapple with anxiety and a tendency to be a bit of a control freak, but there has been progress. Now, I possess the tools I've gained through this transformative process.

I continue to rely on Jesus to lead me along His path. Despite contending with panic and anxiety, I am eternally grateful for discovering a tangible God who has not only transformed my life but also left a lasting impact on my daughter. Now, she witnesses her mother spending quality time with God, speaking positively, and she's developing a resilient and confident attitude in the Lord at her tender age. I feel abundantly blessed that Jesus has reshaped the narrative of my story, breaking chains for my family's future.

Rachel has a God-given gift of relating to and caring for people. She was born and raised in Kansas City, Missouri. She developed her love for Jesus at a young age during the summers she spent with her great-grandparents in Grubbs, Arkansas.

Rachel grew up in several youth groups and participated actively, yet she has battled addiction, abuse, rejection, depression, anxiety, and suicidal thoughts. In her young adult years, she gave time to her church's youth ministry to give back what she had learned. She was an active preacher and leader.

Rachel loves using her story and what she has been through in life to reach all ages. She is a great motivator for the people around her. Her heart is to make sure that everyone knows the pure love of God and how grace can restore every hurt or hangup.

She is an accomplished Certified pediatric hematology and oncology nurse. She has won several awards, including the Nursing Excellence and Guardian Angel.

Chapter 4

(Abun-DANCE): GOD Dances is the meaning

by Renee Manzolillo

The shattered identity

Twenty-one years ago, I embodied assertiveness and a strong will as a child and into early adulthood. I marched to the rhythm of my drum with a clear sense of purpose, unyielding determination, and a refusal to accept "no." Failure, too, was off the table. However, somewhere along the journey, I misplaced my identity.

That competitive junior Olympic gymnast, professional dancer, and movement educator disintegrated on July 2, 2004. I broke my back, a terrifying thing. It felt like a vice wrapped around my lower back and ribcage, my legs folded in slow motion with no feeling of falling to the ground. Time stopped; it was as though I stood outside myself, a silent observer in the suspended animation of the moment, watching the scene unfold.

My injuries comprised my L5, S1, spondylolisthesis, and herniated disc, with accompanying nerve damage. What did this all mean? The doctors warned, "You'll never dance again, let alone teach, do choreography, or even work out."

It would be one of my greatest gifts!

Seventeen doctors recommended spinal fusion, but my gut instinct said "No!"

So, instead, I suffered through multiple therapies until I discovered a Pilates class that fit my rehabilitation needs, IM=X Pilates. Through this modality and theory, I could regulate my level of pain. Through intense training, I learned about spinal elongation, breath support, and stabilization of the ribcage and pelvis to allow for the free movement of my arms and legs. Through this experience, I became a certified IM=X Pilates instructor.

Rebirth through movement

After enduring the relentless challenges of both physical and emotional wounds, the harsh reality confronted my heart. The ache of emotional pain surpassed my injuries, leaving me crushed and robbed of my identity. I became withdrawn, crying every day, feeling sorry for myself, and seeing a physiologist, depressed in emotional, mental and physical pain. I had lost my faith and trust in God! For the longest time, I asked, "Why? Why me?" I couldn't comprehend what was happening.

Then, I was introduced to the Laban Bartenieff Institute for Movement Studies (LIMS) by my modern dance teacher, Doreen Laperdon, a graduate of LIMS and for whom I danced in college. I had everything, or at least I believed so. I didn't explore its vast opportunities and the new things it could offer. But when I began researching other movement endeavors, LIMS always popped up first on Google. Then, I came across the information from years before in my hope chest my grandfather made for me. It was a sign from above. I was searching for this or what I hoped it would be. I took the plunge.

I immersed myself in the introductory courses. Soon, I knew this was where I needed to be. But this manifestation would take some time. In the classroom, I would crawl up in a fetal position, crying and releasing. I understood that I needed to shed the layers of emotional, mental and physical pain to heal.

LIMS also supports projects that use Laban Movement Analysis/Bartenieff Fundamentals (LMA/BF). So, entering into the LMA/BF program, I knew I could shed those layers and understand what LIMS could offer me.

A new perspective

There are so many things I wanted to do that I couldn't because of my injury. I walk, bend, and tie my shoes and other things differently! Most of all, my perception of seeing, hearing, and feeling was as if it were for the first time.

During this time, my cousin, who I love dearly, was diagnosed with autism. As an expert on body movement, my goal was to enrich the lives of special-needs children. For example, as a privately trained Applied Behavioral analyst, a common form of therapy for children with autism, I focus on teaching. Through what I have learned as a dancer and how music and storytelling can help children with autism, I helped my cousin. At 21, with ongoing therapy, he is thriving.

I understand where I am today; what led me to the work of Rudolf Laban and Irmgard Bartenieff? How and why did I look here for a way to stop the pain and suffering? Everything I knew stemmed from movement. That's what I know; that is my passion! I entered this theory and application for guidance, support, and healing for my physical, mental, and emotional pain.

Things happen for a reason, all by design. I trust that God placed an obstacle in my path to impart a more profound lesson: to rise again and use my body in ways that align with a higher purpose.

God gave me a gift to teach movement, maybe not how I thought. He opened my eyes to a world where movement favors healing children in need. He was fine-tuning my skills and preparing me to become a certified movement analyst. I needed to attend to my body and mind to heal. Or maybe he was giving me the gift of both worlds: heal myself as I guide others to heal!

How do LMA/BF concepts and principles support human movement behaviors to shape self and others within the environment?

How do body, effort, shape, and space help our mind, body, and soul communicate and make relationships?

Through self-exploration, supported by LMA/BF theory and application, I have understood that all these occurrences were God's way of molding my identity!

God dances through me!

It's your internal strength and wisdom when you hit those rock bottom moments. The strength of God comes from your soul, the inner light that ignites the way. This glimpse of light was a reminder that what you do is not who YOU are!

Experience makes us who we are and who we will become.

Our identity defines us.

I AM Renee Manzolillo, a guide dedicated to curating consciously designed expressions of the soul. My purpose is to foster a sacred alignment within, enabling your identity to resonate through time and space, embracing the true essence of Abun-DANCE.

I AM creating trust and building relationships, chosen to awaken the spirit within. I am here to physically move as light body energy in a human experience through energetic space and time to break the mold so others may find their purpose.

I AM a woman of empowerment, the curator of my soul's expression, which inspires others. It is a reminder that those who need to hear your story hear you differently. I want my spirit to continue to thrive and be alive in others, especially my three gorgeous boys who inspire me to LIVE as GOD intended, full of LOVE, JOY and Abun -DANCE IDENTITY.

As a mom to three boys and a devoted wife for 27 years, Renee spearhead Breakin Boundaries, a Brooklyn-based brand offering unique Holistic and Therapeutic Wellness Experiences. As the founder and Master Facilitator of Sacred Alignment™, she oversees certification and training for advanced aligned body workers and spiritual individuals.

Renee's diverse professional background includes roles as a Certified Movement Analyst, Master Reiki Practitioner, Shamanic guide (recognized as The Limitless Life Choreographer), dance-fitness instructor, and Business Growth Expansion Specialist (The Boundless Badass BIZ Creator). With over two decades of experience as a private ABA therapist in Autism, she enjoys crafting consciously designed experiences that unite the Breakin Boundaries Sacred Alignment™ Community BIZ and Wellness group.

Chapter 5

A Story of Resilience and Restoration

by Stephanie Meiser

My family had moved to a new city and I had started my sophomore year of high school. Sitting in English class I met David, this handsome boy with strawberry blonde hair and the cutest curly mullet, wearing an Ocean Pacific T-shirt and plaid shorts. It was the late 80s. What can I say? We started officially dating that fall, and by spring I was pregnant. I finished my sophomore year at 16 years old and pregnant.

I went to a small Christian school for most of my school years. Although it was a "Christian" school, the environment that I should have felt safe in was a place where I was routinely bullied and never felt as though I fitted in.

One year, we were required to memorize **Psalms 23: 1-4**, "*The LORD is my shepherd. I shall not be in want. He restores my soul. He guides me in paths of righteousness for his name's sake. Even though I walk through the valley of the shadow of death, I will fear no evil, for you are with me; your rod and your staff, they comfort me.*"

I can still remember the comfort those verses provided as a child. Little did I know then that those verses would carry me through some of the most profound hurt and heartache anyone should ever have to deal with.

Growing up in a house where my father was a functional alcoholic meant covering up what life was like at home. My mom, a believer, made it a point to take us to church and worked tirelessly to give us as much of a normal childhood as possible. As the oldest, I knew what was happening in our home, especially as I got older. I clung tightly to the promises in Psalms 23

Choosing the path

There were life-altering decisions that needed to be made and not easy ones, especially at 16 and 18. That summer, at my dad's request, he and I would spend the day together working through a problem-solving worksheet about my future. Ultimately, it was decided that we would get married that fall. David would go to work full-time, and I would continue schooling at a local school for teen moms. We would each continue living at home with our parents until the wedding. On October 10, 1987, standing seven months pregnant, we were married at our church with our family and friends joining us.

The first few months seemed like a whirlwind. We celebrated our first Christmas and anxiously awaited the birth of our first child. I am now an adult making adult decisions, but I was still a child.

Our son, Derek, was born three months later. I loved being a mom; it was what my heart had always longed for. I knew how to care for a baby. I was the oldest of three and grew up babysitting. However, I am now a wife too. That was a role I needed to learn how to do properly.

A season of struggle and heartbreak

When Derek was four months old, I discovered I was pregnant again.

Exactly 13 months to the day Derek arrived, we welcomed our second son, Bradley, nine days before my 18th birthday. But later that year, Derek, at 22 months old, was called home to heaven. So here I was, 18 years old, married with two children and had the heartbreak of having to bury our firstborn. Psalms 23 helped carry me through. I would often find myself repeating the verses over and over again in my head. God promised to comfort me for His glory and never abandoned me. **(Psalms 23: 4)** I clung to those promises.

Many didn't think we would make it five years, and the statistics weren't in our favor. Our pure stubbornness kept us from giving up on our marriage. Not only were we teenage parents, but we had also lost a child. One more thing we had going against us. But God... God had a bigger plan.

I was holding tight to the promises of God's word. **Jeremiah 29: 11**, *"For I know the plans I have for you," declares the Lord, "plans to prosper you and not to harm you, plans to give you* *hope and a future.*" I would write verses on index cards and place them around where I could see and memorize them. This verse would come full circle several years later.

If I nag him, he'll go

Life as we knew it was hard. Although David was working full-time, the financial burden of supporting a family was difficult. We were just kids ourselves. Neither of us had an example of what a Christian family should be, much less a healthy family unit. In the beginning, we went to church off and on. It slowly became less and less.

After losing Derek, our attendance increased. Later, David took a more supportive role from the outside while I continued attending with Bradley.

During those early years I realized I was the nagging wife. I desired to have a picturesque family, and I thought that by nagging him I would get that "perfect Christian family." I was sorely wrong. It only added to the conflict. I knew something needed to change.

It was during this time that a mentor encouraged me with **1 Peter 3: 1-2**: "*Wives, in the same way, submit yourselves to your husbands so that, if any of them do not believe the word, they may be won over without words by the behavior of their wives, when they see the purity and reverence of your lives.*"

I once again clung to these promises in God's word. I slowly changed my nagging ways. Was I perfect, and did it happen quickly? No, not at all! But God was molding me into the wife I was meant to be.

A new season

Life was moving along, and we're now in our early 20s. Although working part-time, my main focus was being a mom and wife. That's where I was fulfilled and found the most joy. It had been three years since our loss, and we were ready for another baby.

Both of my births hadn't been easy, but our third proved to be the one that would test our faith. There were complications during delivery for both of us. As quickly as I had her in my arms, the nurses took her from me because she wasn't breathing. As the Code Blue rang out, uncertainty filled the room; Morgan needed to be resuscitated. I remember hearing my doctor saying, "I'm not waiting," as he immediately tended to her. It was minutes that felt like a lifetime of thinking we were going to lose another child.

Thankfully, my doctor was able to resuscitate her just before the response team ran into the hospital room. Just as we were settling in, I started experiencing complications from the delivery. During this time, I saw a side of love and care in David that I hadn't experienced before.

Even before we left the hospital, my doctor advised me that it wouldn't be a wise decision to have any more children. The following weeks I was recovering and relishing the blessing of a new birth. I was reminded that no matter our circumstances, we are to be rejoicing in the Lord.

Journey of faith

As the years passed the kids grew, and we grew. At times our marriage was great; other times it was hard. Most Sundays and Wednesdays the kids and I would attend church. Yet, I still yearned for us to go to church together as a family.

I had prayed for God to change David's heart for years and often questioned why that wasn't happening. While attending the Bible study "Experiencing God," I soon realized that I had to change my heart again. One day during our studies, we went outside and had some alone time. It was during that time that I saw the reflection of the church steeple in the pond. God revealed to me that I am the reflection of Christ in my home and my husband. It was me that had to make the change. Once again, **1 Peter 3: 1-2** was brought to life, but this time in a different way.

During those many years of growing in my faith, God again gave me **Jeremiah 29: 11** as a verse to claim. It was his promise to me that one day our family would all attend church together and be baptized as a family. It wasn't overnight, but years later at a Third Day concert, the Holy Spirit took hold of David's heart. What a glorious day that was. God's promises were coming to life, and I saw them unfold. Not long after, we were all baptized as a family, as God had promised me in his Word.

Resilience and restoration

Has the journey been smooth? Certainly not! However, God surpasses any challenge we encounter. Through the years we continued to have heartbreaking situations we've had to deal with, but each time we fought through them. We've faced challenging circumstances that might have led to our downfall if we hadn't clung to our unwavering faith.

We were committed to creating a life different than what we both had growing up. We were committed to breaking the cycle of divorce. God has used our story to encourage and minister to others. He has taken the pain we've been through and brought us closer to him and each other.

God has done work in my heart, in what once would have driven me crazy about David's personality, I've now learned to love. I've embraced our differences and quirks. I've put aside the selfish, nagging, unloving wife I once was and see him as God's gift to me and our family. Now, 36 years into marriage, we enjoy life as empty nesters and are each other's best friends. Our story of resilience and restoration is still being written, knowing that the best is still to come.

It was no accident that, as a young child, I hid Psalms 23 in my heart. It will forever be my promise from God that he is there for me no matter the mountaintop I'm on or the valley I'm in.

I urge you to remember that, regardless of your challenges, you are embraced by a God whose love knows no bounds, desiring only the best for you. The journey may not always be smooth, but rest assured, He pledges His goodness and mercy to you. In moments of solitude and despair, take solace in the assurance that God is actively orchestrating events for your benefit, even during your most difficult times. Hold onto hope, for His promises are steadfast.

Remember, your story is still being written.

Stephanie is the namesake behind the Along Came Stephanie brand. Her career in the event and wedding industry spanned over two decades as she built her boutique planning and design company with clients and events across the globe.

As a certified Life & Mindset Coach and a Functional Beauty Specialist, she now focuses on helping women simplify their lives through holistic living and embrace intentionality in their relationships. Her mission is to help women find their purpose and leave a powerful legacy.

Stephanie resides in Southwest Florida with her husband of over 36 years. She's a proud mother to her two adult children, Bradley and Morgan, and her angel son, Derek.

Chapter 6

Overcoming Adversity: A Journey Through Pain, Surgery, and Loss

by Leslie Smith

Despite physical limitations a fulfilling life is possible. If you've encountered the emotional pain of debilitating surgery and losing a parent during your teenage years, like me, you're not alone. Life's path has many twists and turns, yet they don't shape your worth or accomplishments.

Adapting to change: Life's new normal

"Your lungs seem fine, but is your back hurting?" asked the doctor.

"Yes," I replied. "It hurts to run and walk, but I assumed it was from sleeping on the couch."

The doctor referred me to a spinal specialist. I was only 12 years old. My parents and I went to see the specialist and learned that I had a 49-degree curve in my spine. My muscles were displaced and alternative healing was no longer an option.

Surgery became my only choice. I underwent 10 hours of

surgery during which they placed 14 screws and two rods in my spine. I had to adapt to a new life with physical limitations, relearning how to walk, navigate stairs, dress myself, and move in and out of bed.

Basic tasks became daunting, requiring help using the bathroom and maintaining hygiene. I substituted school classes with physical therapy sessions, relying on a walker or wheelchair for longer distances. I wore an unsightly thick white back brace. Nurses conducted weekly check-ups for wound care and medication.

It became my new normal.

Despite continued therapy, medication, and exercises, the physical pain persisted. After two years of more doctor visits, x-rays, and MRIs, it turned out that my bones had rejected some screws, and they started moving. Therefore, I underwent a second back surgery, then the same healing process and the same pain for another four years.

Expressing my concerns and emotions, I sought a different surgeon for a potential third back surgery. I found a highly rated one and underwent the surgery. Initially estimated at six hours, the operation stretched to 12 hours. The surgeon inserted screws into each hip and fully fused my lower spine.

When I woke up, I cried because of unbearable pain. My nerves spasmed and my foot felt on fire, the burning sensation making me fear it would last forever. Trusting in the healing process became complicated. I longed for simple activities like going to the mall with friends. Thankfully, they supported me, pushing me in my wheelchair wherever we went, but my embarrassment lingered. This surgery was by far the worst mentally. I relied on my dad, close friends, and boyfriend for help. It took about a year to feel somewhat normal again. I fell into a deep depression, gained over a hundred pounds, and relied on strong medication to cope; seeking solace in sleep to alleviate the pain.

Facing the unthinkable

Two weeks before turning 16 and one month away from my second back surgery, my mom was very sick. She had ovarian cancer. The pain this caused my family was heartbreaking. She was super healthy and never smoked or drank alcohol. She walked up to four miles a day.

I watched my petite mother, with her long curly hair, change to swollen body parts, a baldhead, sweatshirts, and sweatpants. We went from her attending my school performances to attending her chemo treatments. Even though she was fighting cancer, she still threw on her wig, went to work, walked on the treadmill, and took care of the household. She was a loving wife to my father and the biggest supporter of my sister and I.

In the middle of one night, I get woken up by tugging on my bed sheets. "I can't breathe," mom tells me. I'm trying to calm her anxiety, and as I see her trying to walk out of the room. Immediately, I jumped out of bed and caught up with her. Then she collapsed in my arms, and we fell together.

I managed to call 911, turned on the porch lights and left the door open for the EMTs. I returned to my mom to find she was foaming at the mouth. I sat her up and tried to keep her head elevated so she didn't choke. The waiting period felt like forever; her weight was getting heavier and her body was twitching.

When the EMTs arrived, they placed her in the ambulance, and I rode with her to the hospital. They rushed her into the emergency room. Everything was such a blur. I contacted my father at work to tell him the news about Mom. He left work and rushed to the hospital. I'm supposed to go to school in a couple of hours.

The next time I see my mom, it's with tubes down her throat. She's sleeping in and out. She's unable to speak, but she can communicate through writing. A few days went by, and she's doing better. She's able to come home. We had a good couple of months until more complications arose. She had more swelling and couldn't keep food down. I remember holding the trash can for her to vomit in. She was becoming weak.

Until one day, my dad received the news that there was nothing more they could do. She was only in hospice for one week before she passed away. I watched her take her last breath. My mom's passing taught me not to take life for granted—you may navigate life perfectly, yet abruptly, it can be shortened. Embrace life purposefully, go on vacations, and express love to everyone around you.

Truancy

Amidst a series of back surgeries and the passing of my mother, my dad began receiving truancy letters. I've been in and out of school since seventh grade, missing so much that it became a significant issue. Attending school regularly became impossible. Although my dad would collect homework packets for me, I consistently struggled to complete them on time.

We tried online schooling. That didn't work. I couldn't concentrate because of the medication. I was failing everything. We met with a school counselor, who said if I kept going at that rate, I would be a super senior. Meaning I wouldn't graduate until I turned 21. My dad and I agreed I'd drop out after my sixteenth birthday and enroll in community college under the early admission program. I took the placement test and scored high enough to attend college-level courses.

My mother strongly influenced my choice to pursue nursing, so I enrolled in medical terminology and took fun electives for my artistic side. I loved photography and baking. At sixteen, I wasn't sure what I wanted to do with my life, but once I started studying those confusing medical terms, I said nope, not for me.

I had a passion for the arts.

I took drawing, photography, and some baking classes. Baking was very therapeutic, and I soon graduated with my associate's degree in Pastry Arts. From there, I had a five-year bakery business that served its purpose in my life—I met the best of friends who showed me faithful support, was able to express my creativity, and learned hard lessons. I could influence others that one didn't need to graduate high school to be successful.

Years later and nursing keeps popping up in my head, and I usually take these signs of guidance from my angels. Out of curiosity, I explored my options. I found a program nearby that fit my needs to make it even possible. I studied hard and passed the entrance exam. After the interview with the nursing program director, I received an acceptance letter into the program.

I'm embarking on the next chapter of my life. Refuse to let life's unfortunate events shape your future, as anything is possible. I hold a strong belief in divine timing.

Don't allow challenging circumstances to define your destiny. Take control as you step into the next phase of your life. Whether dealing with physical limitations, coping with loss, or overcoming educational obstacles, trust in divine timing and envision a rewarding and prosperous future.

Born on March 21st, 1997, in a small town outside of Detroit, Michigan, Leslie is a highly motivated individual who has overcome many challenges in her life. She has always been goal-oriented and driven to succeed, pushing herself to be the best she can be.

Despite obstacles, Leslie has remained focused on her goals, and her determination has helped her achieve many successes. Leslie is a devoted wife to her husband, with whom she shares a love of travel and adventure, traveling around the world and immersing themselves in new cultures and experiences.

Leslie finds travel to be a way to expand her horizons and gain a deeper understanding of the world around her. In her free time, Leslie enjoys gardening, cooking, and baking. Gardening is a therapeutic activity that allows her to connect with nature and enjoy simple pleasures.

She enjoys experimenting with new recipes and baking delicious treats for her loved ones. Leslie's diverse experiences have given her a unique perspective on life. She remains committed to positively impacting the world around her and helping others achieve their goals. Her unwavering determination and kind and caring spirit continue to inspire those who know her, making her a true role model and inspiration.

Chapter 7

Divorce, Dead Birds, and Divine Guidance

by Kelly Lanes

"How did I even get here?"

"How did I allow this to happen to me?"

"Dear God, please have me not hit my head on the ground."

I wondered as I lay looking up at the clouds, full of shock, unable to move, paralyzed by fear.

Five minutes earlier...

*

I was meeting virtually with a long-time client at my home office. The meeting was going swimmingly when suddenly, the door burst open. My husband is panting and keeps repeating, "I need your help! I need your help!" I was taken aback, as our household had an unspoken understanding that we preferred not to be disturbed if our office doors were closed.

The look on my face told my client enough that I apologized, closed the meeting, and rushed out of my office. All I could think of was, "What happened to my dog?"

As we run outside, I get more nervous about my dog! I am almost in tears as I ask, "Where's Ranger? Is he okay?"

I was running behind my husband in the backyard, and he stopped and turned to me to say, "I think Ranger's on the couch; he's fine."

I felt confused but followed anyway. I thought, "What is this rush about?"

We reached the backyard. My husband ushered me to a large terracotta pot and said, "Help me move this back onto the deck, will you?"

I looked at him in disarray and said, "Are you serious right now? I thought something terrible had happened! I canceled an important meeting to help you move this pot?"

He looked back at me as if I had no right to question his needs and judgment and said, "Well, you're out here now. Will you help me move this?"

I let out an audible sigh but thought that I might as well help him now.

This wasn't the first, second or one-hundredth time I had stopped my life to do something for him. I always felt that his world was always more important than mine, and after almost 10 years, this was just another instance.

So I brace myself as I try my best to squat down between other lawn equipment and furniture and lift the pot to where he wanted it. It took about 20 seconds before I suggested, "We should try to drag this instead; it's too heavy to lift."

This caused some sort of rage in my husband, and he exclaimed, "Never mind, you're worthless; I'll f***ing do it myself!" And he shoved me out of the way. He pushed me so hard that all I could remember was praying not to hit my head on the rocks as I fell backwards, but luckily I landed on the ground.

*

"How did I get here?"

All I knew at that moment was that I needed to leave. Leave my house right then and make a plan for a path forward. I got up from the ground slowly with a fuzzy head and a heavy heart and I looked at him, and while holding back tears I yelled, "Screw you!" I ran inside. I checked on our animals. He was right; the dog was safe on the couch, and the cats were hidden in their hiding places.

I packed my work bag and keys and headed to my favorite cafe for the rest of the day. I didn't want to see any friends or family, so I went to my happy place. Coffee always soothes me, brings me joy and provides me a safe space.

Luckily, my favorite cafe near my house is open late, so I could indulge in multiple lattes and decaf cups of coffee and distract myself until 10 p.m. before heading home.

*

All I could do was wake up, thank God for what I had, drink excellent coffee, focus on the business that brings me joy, serve others who bring me joy, and listen to my gut and my inner knowledge from God.

A month after what I call "the incident," we were in couple's therapy. Since that fateful day I had stopped sleeping in the same bed, much less on the same floor of our house as my husband. I would wake up crying most nights, thinking that he would get white with rage again and hurt me more. I couldn't be within feet of him without shaking or crying or running away.

In one of our sessions, the therapist asked me to explain what I kept referring to as "the incident." I referred to it as our relationship before and after the incident.

After explaining and struggling to get through it without completely breaking down, the therapist asked my husband, "Does this story align with what you remember?" He responded, "I don't remember this happening at all."

I knew I couldn't stay. I couldn't stay with a man who couldn't even remember hurting me, couldn't remember shoving me or irrationally making me do what he needed. My gut was screaming at me. And for the first time I listened to it and didn't push that feeling aside.

*

After the therapy session I sat on my backyard patio, journaling and praying alone. I looked up from the pages and noticed some random clump of something. I walked over to it to grab it before my dog found it. I realized it was a dead bird.

I had been journaling about how I think it's a good idea to leave my husband. I prayed God would give me a sign to gain clarity from Him to see the lies and anxious activity. The trust issues and the abuse had gone too far for me. Looking at this dead bird, I wondered, "What does this mean? This has to be a sign." After doing what any sensible woman would do (a.k.a. Googling what it means), the definition shook me to my core.

To paraphrase what Google said... "It may signify the end of something significant in our lives, leaving us discontented and lost. The death of a bird can also symbolize change and transformation. It serves as a reminder that to experience renewal and growth, we must let go of the past."

I cried, and I prayed thanks to God and asked for strength. That next day was the day I told my husband that I wanted a divorce. There was no magical romance novel ending. He didn't even fight it when I told him. Within 30 minutes, he had all our assets split up on a spreadsheet for who was getting what, right down to our three beloved pets!

The month after we sold our house, I moved into a 600-square-foot farm apartment with no heat and brought both cats. It was here that I found true solace for the first time in my adult life. We shared custody of our dog for a while, and every time I had to give him back, my heart broke more and more. Once the divorce date came we met over Zoom with the judge, and I remember the judge calling me by my maiden name again and asking how it sounded. I started crying, thinking, "It sounded like relief and a new start."

*

God doesn't place things on your heart by accident.

Each little nudge he gives you pushes you toward your dreams, and His will for you is sometimes what He wants, not what you want, and that's where conflict comes in.

When you ask God for support, signs, and clarity, you might just get it. And it's in that moment that you do nothing but take faithful, joyful action in what He has called you to do, no matter how scary or uncomfortable it may be. God has bigger plans for me, and he has bigger plans for you too.

You just have to be ready to listen to him.

Over three years I transitioned from getting engaged, navigating through the challenges of COVID-19, resigning from my job, initiating one business venture, tying the knot, launching a second business, experiencing a divorce, discovering my path, facing setbacks, and relocating across the country to rediscover my direction.

The common denominator is how God was there, no matter how dark it got or what challenges I faced. He placed me in those moments to show me something. To frame me into who I am today.

Had I succumbed to fear and clung to a small controlled version of myself from the past, I wouldn't currently be perfectly placed in my dream apartment in my dream city, living out my dreams.

Regardless of where you stand on the journey to discovering daily freedom and joy, refrain from allowing your imperfect past to obstruct your blessed future.

Was leaving my husband hard? Yes!

Was selling my house and moving across the country hard? Yes!

Was choosing joy every day hard? Yes!

Was growing hard? Yes!

But nothing is as painful as being in a situation that is against God's plan and not serving you.

I chose God and went all in on the path he was placing me on.

The key to happiness is hard work and faith. It's finding and choosing joy every day, even in darkness. It's knowing that you've done everything possible to listen to God's plan for you and take faithful and relentless action. It's remembering to buy a latte for the person behind you in line at your local coffee shop because you never know what people are going through, and smiles are contagious.

If you feel God is nudging you to do something, your faith will help you make that happen.

Feeling into faith will support you when the going gets tough.

Feeling into faith serves others more than yourself.

Feeling into faith shows you that no matter what needs to get done, you have the inner strength to do it.

Coffee always helps this process too!

Where your discomfort lies is also where your greatest accomplishments may lie.

No matter what you're going through, I pray you know God has you placed in the exact spot and time you're supposed to. Whether you're lying on your back looking at the sky or sitting in your favorite place with a caffeinated beverage, you are perfectly placed.

Kelly Lanes, a dedicated advocate of strategic thinking and positivity, believes she can contribute positivity to the world—one cup of coffee at a time. Demonstrating unwavering commitment, Kelly radiates positive vibes and shares her marketing insights with clients and the global audience.

With an impressive 10-plus years in marketing, Kelly is a renowned speaker on diverse subjects such as marketing strategies, positivity, and the significance of authenticity. Her mission is to inspire and empower individuals through compelling discussions, leveraging her extensive knowledge and practical experience in the field.

She expresses gratitude daily, thanking God for guiding her through trials and triumphs and recognizing the importance of each experience in shaping her journey. This deep connection with faith is a source of strength and resilience, infusing purpose into every aspect of Kelly's life.

Chapter 8

From Breakup to Breakthrough

by Avarel M. Smith

Shattered vows

In 2018, life bestowed upon me the status of a divorcee—a label burdened with the weight of shattered dreams and a concluded chapter. However, within the debris of a fractured union, I unearthed the seeds of resilience, purpose, and an unforeseen journey that would guide me toward the transformative role of a dating coach.

When my ex-husband told me I was "acting like a b*tch," I knew my relationship was over. I had never been called that to my face. While it might be expected that women could be subjected to derogatory names from their spouses, this was foreign to me.

It was more about principle than anything else. He disrespected me after one of his family members came to our home and said the same thing. I decided she wasn't welcomed back, and he was outraged. That was my "red flag" of what else to expect.

"You teach people how to treat you by what you allow, what you stop and what you reinforce."—Tony Gaskins.

A spiritual awakening

I stood at the crossroads of despair and possibility. Instead of succumbing to the weight of heartache, I redefined my narrative. This decision laid the foundation for a journey that would see me morph from a divorced soul to a guiding light for women.

Daily prayer became my anchor during my tumultuous divorce. There were days when he tried to provoke a response out of me. However, my faith gave me solace and strength to face the challenges head-on, the courage to embrace vulnerability, and the resilience to keep moving forward.

We all have a God-given inner strength and sometimes must dig deep to find and harness it. God designed us all for a purpose here on earth. He creates paths in our lives, and we must choose which one to take. The threads of our life experiences play a vital role in sculpting our future because we each encounter adversity and confront challenges along the journey. What matters is how we handle them.

Overcoming fear of judgment

The fear of judgment is a painful reality many women grapple with. Sadly, it causes some of them to stay married to avoid being labeled. That's because society often places an unwarranted stigma on divorced individuals, and women are particularly unfairly judged. In a 2014 HuffPost article, The

Divorcee Stigma That's Alive And Well, D.A. Wolf, the creator of Daily Plate of Crazy, wrote, "The way out of this particular bind, it would seem, is via remarriage. And if you haven't somehow compensated for divorce by walking down the aisle a second time, you're regarded with suspicion, pity, or at the very least—bewilderment." Societal expectations perpetuate a narrative of failure or inadequacy.

I pondered whether to go through with the divorce. However, there came a liberating moment when I stopped caring about the judgments and opinions of others. I found strength in authenticity, realizing that my story had the power to inspire and uplift other women.

So, I embarked on a journey of self-discovery. Little did I know that this path would lead to healing and becoming a beacon of hope for countless women seeking healing and transformation in their love lives.

A Phoenix rising

I went through a range of emotions, from anger to feeling hurt, to rediscovering my strength, and even from uncertainty to clarity. I held it together, especially for my teenage son. There were rough days when I couldn't fathom this was my new reality. On those days, my commute to work was tearful, yet I would dry my eyes and smile before walking into my office.

Life after divorce presented me with a choice: to let the experience make me or break me. I chose resilience over despair, growth over stagnation, and empowerment over victimhood. My journey is a testament to the transformative power of choice, encouraging women to embrace their agency in shaping their destinies. I turned pain into purpose, and my mess became my message.

Answering the call

In March 2019, the Universe played its cards right into my hands. I learned of a conference in NYC highlighting relationship experts from across the world. I jetted to the Global Love Institute and, over several days, connected with many relationship coaches and matchmakers, some of whom have developed into beautiful friendships.

It was the breakthrough I needed. So, I returned and completed an extensive program and became a certified dating and relationship coach. The idea of becoming a coach seemed ludicrous at first. It meant exposing my journey to the scrutiny of the outside world.

However, I discovered a reservoir of wisdom within myself—lessons learned from my mistakes, victories forged from the fires of heartbreak, and the resilience to rise stronger from the ashes of my past.

Transforming love lives

Through coaching, I've realized my profound impact on women's lives. Each client brings a unique set of challenges and fears, some mirroring the ones I once faced. Through empathetic guidance and a genuine understanding of the pain accompanying heartbreak, I started transforming love lives one heart at a time.

My clients' stories have become testimonials to the power of healing, converting pain into a driving force for positive change. They have started their dating journey with mindset mastery and increased self-love, self-confidence, and self-worth. They know who and what they want while learning how to set healthy boundaries. Their self-sabotaging beliefs are tossed out to sea, and they release any lingering emotional baggage from past relationships.

My dating blueprint helps them attract the right partner and understand what fundamental life values are important to them. Mastering the art of communication, uncovering powerful strategies to build trust, and resolving conflict constructively, are part of their arsenal to ensure a successful relationship.

A future of possibilities

Before becoming a coach, I co-owned a small matchmaking company in the Atlanta area. However, I quickly realized I wanted sole business ownership. So, in June 2019, I became the founder & CEO of Seeking Synergy.

Since relationships and finances go hand in hand, I also chose to become a licensed insurance agent in November 2020.

Now, I help individuals protect their families while building generational wealth.

In November 2023, I became the bestselling author of "Everyday Woman's Guide to Living Your Best Life" and co-authored it with 31 incredible women from diverse backgrounds. My chapter, "Unlocking Your Communication Potential," delves into becoming a "Captain Communicator," a "Conflict Conqueror" and a "Tenacious Trust Builder" in relationships.

I'm channeling my experience and knowledge into a purpose-driven career. Embracing the challenge of helping other women navigate the complexities of dating and relationships has been rewarding. Empowering and educating them to stop normalizing toxicity in their relationships and lives has become my passion. I believe toxicity is the heroin of relationships.

Rooted in purpose

I am right where I'm supposed to be at this season of my life. I've been perfectly placed in the dating and relationship arena, doing God's work and transforming love lives.

My feet are planted on solid ground. I'm focused on the mission at hand. Through prayer and a lot of soul-searching, I've found myself. I'm highly confident, know my true self-worth, continuously give myself grace, love the woman I am, and feel blessed that I'm becoming the best version of myself.

I can now be the vessel God has chosen to help women envision, embrace and, most importantly, experience a healthy relationship.

Beyond divorce: A new chapter

By the grace of God, and when I wasn't even looking or expecting it, I met a wonderful man.

He's perfect for me. We've agreed to take things slow as both of us are divorced. We've discussed what we wanted the dynamics of our marriage to be. It has been an incredible journey, applying everything I've learned to ensure our relationship has trust, communication, honesty, respect, healthy boundaries, love and understanding. We are mutually responsible for our happiness.

God's grace = Your power

Within God's grace lies an incredible source of our strength. So, while you may draw inspiration and guidance from this spiritual realm, the ability to tap into your divine strength ultimately becomes your source of power. Each experience, whether tough days or moments of clarity, becomes an opportunity to lean on your courage, which is divinely instilled in each of us.

I proudly declare myself an "Overcomer," having navigated the stormy seas of divorce and emerged stronger, wiser, and more attuned to my faith, which has sustained me. Faith is the Victory!

I invite you to recognize your God-given inner strength—a beacon guiding you through the darkest nights and into the dawn of a new chapter. You will not just survive but emerge as a triumphant "Overcomer," shaping your story with an empowered quill.

Remember, within you lies a force that transforms challenges into stepping stones.

Avarel Smith, aka the Toxicity to Authenticity Coach®, is the Founder/CEO of Seeking Synergy, a Certified Dating & Relationship Coach, and a former Matchmaker. She is committed to helping single women navigate the intricacies of modern dating and relationships.

Avarel focuses on dismantling toxic patterns, fostering genuine connections, embracing authenticity, confidently navigating the dating landscape, and cultivating healthy relationships. To help them do so, she educates them on self-love, mindset mastery, effective communication, building trust, and conflict resolution.

She is a bestselling author of Everyday Woman's Guide To Living Your Best Life, which she co-authored with 31 other entrepreneurs of diverse backgrounds.

Chapter 9

From Shadows to Strength

by Katharine Parry

As a child, the storms raging within my home shaped my life, and I believed no one outside could see them. By the time I was seven, my father's casual drinking had morphed into an all-consuming addiction, casting shadows that stretched far beyond our family's doorstep.

Financial struggles became our silent companion. My parents wrestled with the weight of my dad's problems. Although my parents worked hard every week, a significant amount of money went towards his addiction. My mom struggled to keep things afloat and did extra jobs, from bookkeeping to cleaning houses and making Christmas wreaths or painting trucks for my grandfather. Despite never wanting for love or support, the turbulence of their arguments, financial insecurities and my dad's broken promises formed the backdrop of my childhood.

I yearned for my mom to break free, to start anew or for my dad to find the courage to face his problem. My diaries, filled with pleas for her to leave or for him to stop drinking, were my silent confidants. The unpredictability of my dad's demeanor became a haunting uncertainty, especially as he struggled to stop drinking repeatedly. I can vividly recall an instance where he and my mom got into an argument about him lying to conceal that he had been drinking.

He drove away with a gun in hand while screaming that he was going to burn the house down. I hid in the closet with tears streaming down my face while holding my little sister tight, thinking he would end up killing my mom or himself. Shame became a quiet companion, urging me to hide the scars of my dad's addiction from the world. The facade of normalcy became my armor, concealing the turmoil within.

But, by the grace of God, a turning point arrived. My dad, driven by an internal awakening, decided "enough." But the scars of my childhood carried a profound purpose. Conflict resolution became a skill honed amid my parents' disagreements. They had been through dark times together when they were at a crossroads, but they stayed together and worked through their problems.

They showed me how to navigate conflict, hold difficult conversations, bounce back, and move forward. I witnessed the corrosive impact of addiction on families, learning the painful truth that change must begin with you. I learned at a young age that recognizing a problem is the first step in seeking help. Embracing the imperfections in my parents was a pivotal step toward self-acceptance as a parent myself. Recognizing that perfection is an unattainable standard, I find solace in the understanding that, just like them, I am beautifully imperfect in my parenthood journey.

I see the purpose in my pain. My shadow transformed into a source of strength, guiding me through the intricate roles of motherhood, marriage and entrepreneurship. I found resilience in the shadow's depths. In pain, I discovered purpose.

Amidst the storms

Life has continued to present me with formidable challenges including wrestling with self-doubts and immense pressure to achieve my success, facing anxiety that tightened its grip at different times, and confronting the overwhelming storm of postpartum depression after the birth of both my children. Its weight nearly shattered the foundations of my marriage. I found myself in a relentless cycle of tears and anger, emotions that seemed to erupt over the slightest provocations.

Yet, amidst the storms of anxiety and postpartum depression, my husband and I poured our hearts and souls into our farm and built two businesses through years of hard work, resilience, and sacrifice. It stings when others assume it happened overnight or that success came on a silver platter.

We have faced our doubts, stumbled, and picked ourselves up. We have seen the beauty in the struggle and the growth that comes from overcoming adversity, just as I witnessed in my parents. This journey is as authentic as it gets. It is about pushing through and proving that we can achieve our dreams through sheer grit and passion.

Yet, beneath every accomplishment there was a constant pull—an insatiable need to prove my worth—a deeply ingrained habit from childhood observing the financial success of other family members. Striving to achieve, outshine, and outperform became a way of showing my worthiness; people-pleasing that danced in the shadows of my actions. I chased success because I grew up in an environment where achievement made me feel seen and loved by the people I admired.

I discovered that self-worth undergoes a profound transformation when I consciously stripped away layers of ingrained conditioning, casting off the notion that my value relied on achievements, accolades, or constant approval from others;, known as unlearning—untangling the threads of external expectations woven into the fabric of my self-perception.

The shadows of people-pleasing, born in childhood, dissipated as I embraced the authentic core of my being. This awakening was not a rejection of ambition or personal growth but the redefinition of my parents' purpose. No longer were they driven by a hunger for validation but by a genuine desire for self-improvement and fulfillment.

With this newfound perspective, I navigated life's challenges not to prove my worth but as opportunities for growth, learning, and embracing my authentic self. The need to outshine others faded, replaced by a commitment to shine my light, regardless of external comparisons.

In embracing self-worth from within, I found freedom. The weight of expectations lifted, allowing me to move through life with a genuine sense of purpose, unburdened by the shackles of validation-seeking; a homecoming to my true self, where worthiness is recognized and celebrated as an inherent birthright.

Sharing my truth

There is immense power in sharing our stories. Each narrative and revelation becomes a lifeline for someone barely holding on. The value of storytelling lies not just in personal liberation but also in becoming a thread of connection for those silently grappling with similar struggles—ones that go on behind closed doors or the façade of normalcy.

Sharing my truth is about exposing wounds and illuminating the path for others stumbling in the dark. In those moments of raw authenticity we become beacons, guiding others through their storms.

Amidst the shadows I learned to set boundaries, recognizing that my well-being mattered too, especially when dealing with other family members or friends who have battled addiction issues. Self-awareness became a guiding light, helping me identify my triggers and transcend their impact. Diving into self-awareness tools like human design and exploring my love language has provided valuable insights into who I am, why I am this way, and how I love and want love in return.

Making time for myself and with the people I love is equally important. Prioritizing moments alone allows me to recharge, finding solace and strength within. Simultaneously, nurturing connections with loved ones allows me to see others deeply and live in a community with one another the way God intended us to do.

I discovered the importance of self-compassion, a light within the shadows. It was not just about weathering storms but treating myself with kindness in the aftermath. Meditation and visualization have become a daily practice that anchors me in the present, providing a refuge from the chaos.

Embark on this transformative journey, a call to action in the ongoing pursuit of self-discovery and self-love. Take each step away from the shadow of external validation as a powerful stride toward authentic living. Let go of the belief that your worth is tied to constant achievement or proving yourself. Your scars don't define you; inherently you are enough.

Recognize that you are more than the pain you've endured. In the crucible of difficult times, discover a steadfast companion—grit. Remember, YOU are enough.

Katharine
PARRY

Scan to connect with Katharine

Katharine Parry is a multi-passionate woman who wears many hats. She is a Storyteller, Farmer, and Insurance professional, Theta Reiki Master and operates several small businesses with her husband, Evan.

Beyond these roles, her most rewarding title is being a mother to her two young children. Embracing the wisdom gained from continuous years of self-discovery, reflection, and inner work, she decided to share her journey and empower others to find their voice. Connect with Katharine through her website or social networks for a transformative experience.

Chapter 10

Different Face, Same heart

by Anna Mae Neddie

"The only person you are destined to become is the person you decide to be."
—Ralph Waldo Emerson.

Going through the motions

"Nothing will work unless you do."
—Maya Angelou.

Failure is a universal experience. The crucial factor lies in the intensity of the setback and whether you use it as a learning opportunity or continue to face repeated failures. Those failing moments will eventually lead to life's most significant strengths and growth.

I'm a work in progress. In the assessment of many, I have been successful. Everything looks great on paper: married, a gorgeous family and great friends. Even my hobbies, cooking, entertaining, and attending church, look good. The beautiful smiles on social media depict a thriving young, dynamic lady. But I had been losing myself for a long time and didn't notice until things came crashing down. It suffocated me.

I was afraid, to be honest, afraid of admitting that I had lost myself, and avoided confronting the issues destroying me on the inside. It had been a few years since I'd told myself that all was well. Each night, I would pray unrelentingly for clarity and understanding. With everything looking good to the outside world, how could someone have all these fears and emotions? How could someone who prayed to God and was faithful to family and community be sad and empty?

Was I overlooking something? Did I have high expectations of myself? I'm very critical of myself and always strived to improve, but it was more than that. I had ignored many things that were haunting me.

I wanted to understand how to be better as a wife, an employee, a mother, a friend, and a daughter. The list went on, but there was one person I ignored—myself.

I prayed to understand the different roles I played and worked hard at. But I ignored what God was telling me about who He created me to be and my purpose. I thought I was living out my purpose in these various roles that I was blessed to have. I dug deeper and kept giving of myself, hoping something would change.

It would take me a long time to realize that I needed to make a difference in my life through joy and living beyond any limitations imposed by society, culture, class, family, and self-doubt. I needed to break through and create certain boundaries and healthy rules of engagement, whether spoken or unspoken, and I needed to lose those subtle norms that held me back. Absolute joy comes from God and is ours forever. That joy transforms and regenerates. It is deeply rooted and inspires contentment, and I would have to take on a different face with the same heart to start living joyfully.

Going through the fire

"If it is important to you, you will find a way. If not, you will find an excuse. Too many of us are not living our dreams because we are living our fears." — Les Brown.

Fear has two meanings: (F)orget (E)verything (A)nd (R)un, or (F)ace (E)verything (A)nd (R)ise. The choice is ours. It seems easy to forget and run, but the truth is that you'll never forget because you haven't come to terms with forgiving yourself for the letdown. The downside is that running will haunt you for the rest of your life and becomes cemented in regret, pity, and remorse.

It all came crashing down when I accepted a new role and had to relocate my family for the new job. It wasn't the first move in my life, but this move was going to make or break me. It was the beginning of 2022, and I had been in the thick of applying for various jobs. Several months later, I received a tentative offer requiring me to move my family out of state. There were many unknowns. We'd have to sell our home to consider purchasing another. The kids had eight weeks to enroll in school and couldn't engage in summer activities because of state requirements. So much was riding on getting a home and re-establishing ourselves. We navigated the Airbnb scene for six of those eight weeks, moving four more times. I felt miserable for my kids. I felt the burden of everyone's discomfort. It seemed like everything was my fault because the move revolved around my career.

Whenever I attempted to share my thoughts and plans with my spouse, I never felt listened to or validated, just like in childhood. In every conversation, I could hear and feel the frustration of the changes piercing me with harsh, high tones and irritability from a "higher-up." I was operating on autopilot, and things only got worse. I dug deeper into my self-reliance and FEAR—Forget Everything And Run! I was spiraling and wanted to give up.

I started feeling sorry for myself, living in regret. I soon wished we hadn't moved or left my old job. If we had never moved, I would have been comfortable in my old home, and everything would have been fine. I was lying to myself. Things were far from perfect before. I was miserable and had intentionally been ignoring my pain.

I felt unsupported and was already struggling. So, I would take on everything, feeling alone and angry. In my head, you just roll up your sleeves and do some dirty work! That was how I rolled! Everything had been breaking down, but I would still attend church and be functional for the world. I was not working for ME. Things kept disintegrating in every way, every day. The kids could feel it; we could all feel it. I was working hard on all fronts, trying to change outlooks and be better for everyone.

By the end of September 2023, I was examining my life and broke down. I was sad for several hours, sobbing and bawling at times. I came to terms with my pain, my brokenness and my inability to create healthy boundaries to protect myself from what I had been surviving. I had never chosen myself before. I lived for everyone: my spouse, friends, siblings, parents, children, church community—you name it. At various stages in my life, I was always choosing others and never myself. I felt so broken and so empty. But then my FEAR went from fleeing and running to Facing Everything And Rising. I was humbled.

Loving yourself

"Healing also means taking an honest look at the role you play in your own suffering."—Unknown.

By the end of October 2023, I understood that we facilitate things without knowing how they would impact us negatively later. So, I came to terms with who I was, what I had allowed myself to be, and how I intended to live my life moving forward. I called this progress!

I have listened to podcasts about failure. I have accepted that I only become a failure when I stop working to become the best version of myself. There are many different quotes about failure, and one that strikes me most is Alex Lieberman of the Founder's Journal, who said, "The only true failure is inaction.

Inaction due to laziness. Or inaction due to fear. Everything else is education."

I grew up being dependable and self-reliant. Looking back on my childhood, I frequently faced pressure to excel, driven by the fear of failure if I didn't heed advice. This fear however, instilled a deep anxiety about failing, which persisted into adulthood. The apprehension of the unknown and discomfort with challenging situations became ingrained traits in adulthood.

Fortunately, several scriptures always come to mind when I feel challenged. I often recite parts, starting with the first two verses, then always proceeding to "ye I walk through the valley of the shadow of death, I shall fear no evil for thy rod and staff comfort me." **(Psalm 23: 4)**.

Or Isaiah, who reminds us in verse 40: 31 that we shall soar on wings like eagles and run and not grow weary. However, worn out, all that kept coming to me was one verse I first learned as a seven-year-old, from **Jeremiah 29: 11**, "For I know the plans I have for you," declares the Lord, "plans to prosper you and not harm you, plans to give you hope and a future."

I learned this scripture as a song. I always felt comforted and hopeful for a better tomorrow. It is proof of destiny and the confirmation of purpose. He has called ME by name, and I am His. I had to reaffirm who I was, Who's I was, and what had been spoken to me by my maker.

It went off like a light bulb. "God's got me!" I was determined to get out of my staleness. I would either work on the relationship blessed in covenant or let it go with peace. I had to accept that I was worth making time for.

Accepting you—(Y)our (O)wn (U)niqueness, the whole YOU, the package you were created and wrapped in, from the inside out, is the only way to reach for what you need, sort out what you require, and begin to walk in and fulfill your God-given purpose. It's the only way to be perfectly placed and planted where your feet are. Purpose nourishes the soul, provides direction, and yields high doses of inner satisfaction, value, and self-worth.

Commit to staying the course

We sometimes hit rock bottom, but rebuilding and emerging stronger is crucial. Despite the difficulty, it's work we cannot avoid. I confronted myself and prioritized my well-being. Remember, it's essential not to neglect yourself. There's no reward or recognition for suppressing your emotions or sacrificing your joy to fulfill the expectations of being a "good" daughter, mother, or spouse.

Different face, same heart! It's a new dawn! I came to terms with the truth. My FEAR had me living a life of just getting by. The same heart was still there. I had to love myself and know that I was enough. You can't love God and not love yourself.

To be at peace with God, we need to love ourselves. He is in us and cannot shine within if we are harboring fear, regret, or lack of self-worth. When we start living joyfully, peace comes next, and we feel the assurance of knowing God's goodness. We also feel His presence and know that He is with us.

When peace and harmony are yours, you are perfectly placed where your feet are.

Maatsi NDINGWAN

MAATSINN

Scan to connect with Maatsi

(ANNA MAE NEDDIE)

Maatsi was born in the US, moved to the West Coast, visited Jamaica and then moved to Cameroon before age three. At 17, she returned to the US and attended Clark University in Worcester, MA. Maatsi graduated with a degree in Environmental Science and Policy and a minor in Biology, and later with a graduate degree in Environmental Science & Policy.

Since 2007, Maatsi has worked as an environmental scientist within government institutions. She's a storyteller who brings the often ignored aspects of relationships, life experiences and navigating personal struggles into the spotlight. With a career in environmental policy and management, Maatsi brings a level of authenticity to her storytelling that is both raw and compelling. She has several collections of poems and short stories and has a variety of writing projects underway. Her debut as a co-author in Perfectly Placed: Be Where Your Feet Are channels resilience, spiritual/emotional growth, and character while facing transitions and tribulations.

Maatsi currently resides in Maryland but considers Georgia home, where she is married and raising two children. She volunteers for several organizations: Soup Kitchen, GAP ministry, Meals on Wheels, the local food bank, Golden Harvest, and participates in the Miracle Mile Walk Breast Cancer Foundation.

Chapter 11

The Weight of Water

by Jami Kolev

It was the lowest I have ever been.

I hate this bathroom floor. To this day, I can still feel the icy chill of the linoleum underneath me. My legs cramp as I lean against the wall, unable to stretch out my legs within the tiny space. The ache inside my stomach begged for rest. The dizziness slowly took over my whole body. The smell of the toilet water is just a foot from me. The taste of vomit lingers in my mouth.

It wasn't supposed to be like this. I can't imagine what people would think if they saw me here. I was supposed to succeed—the smart one. And yet, I know I will always find myself here at the end of the day. Knowing it will probably ruin my life if it doesn't kill me first.

An unspoken truth

I don't feel like there was a defining moment growing up when I was like, "Oh, I'm not one of the pretty girls." It's just something I feel like I kind of always knew—an unspoken truth. Growing up in the 2000s, it was kind of everywhere. It was the ideal stick-thin body, and that's not what I had with my soft belly and chunky legs. Not to mention, I had buckteeth growing up. And even after I got braces, I felt like maybe I carried that image in my mind.

I only had one boyfriend growing up. I dated other guys from high school but only had little experience with a real relationship. So, when I met my ex-husband at 18 years old, I was enamored. He was eight years older than me. More mature. More experienced in relationships. And he was looking forward to getting married. Finding a Christian guy with the same belief system made sense for someone who grew up in the church, fully engulfed in this idea that true love waits.

We had our first date at a coffee shop. We talked for hours, which is funny because I only remember two things he said. First, he asked me if I was okay with getting married young. He wanted to get remarried and have kids by age 30. Second, he told me he had always assumed his wife would be into fitness, just like him.

I was so afraid of immediately turning off this mature guy that I played both off like they were no big deal.

Afraid to get married young? Have kids? Not me!

I can't recall my answer to the second question, but he stuck around. And the question stuck with me—the one that changed my life.

At the time, I wasn't into fitness or athletics. I was a terrible athlete growing up, and does anyone really like sit-ups? But out of fear of losing him, I ran a few times a week.

In the first few months, I did great. I started to lose weight, eat healthier, and cut out the broke college student staple of McDonald's and Ramen. And I lost 20 pounds. But then something changed.

We had gone up to Breckenridge to lead worship for our small church retreat. While there, we ate a lot of junk food, pasta, and Mary's Mountain Cookies. The last morning, I looked in the mirror and could feel the bloat from all that food. I was disgusted.

After that, it was a downhill spiral. I started working out at the gym more. Finding time to get an hour of cardio in the morning, 30 minutes at lunch, and even head back after work or school. Every break at school, I went to the gym and worked out more and more, trying to burn a thousand calories a day at the bare minimum. I was obsessed, but I started to see a plateau at some point.

My body had probably reached its maximum weight loss, but in my mind, I might as well have been gaining weight. So, I got more restrictive. I got by on Special K bars throughout the day and maybe a salad for dinner. Eventually, that became a can of chicken broth and green beans, which was the ultimate dinner in my book, coming in at a whopping 50 calories.

And then came the night that I'll never forget.

My dad had brought home some chips and queso (you know, the store-bought Tostino's crap that you know is not made with real cheese). And let me tell you, I indulged. My stomach was physically hurting from how much I ate. We cleaned out the entire jar.

That night, I went to take a shower. The water poured over me, and I felt the weight, the weight of the water, the weight of guilt, and the weight of it all in my stomach. All I wanted was to go back in time like it never happened. All I wanted was to change what I had done. All I wanted was to get it out of my body.

And so it began

It began that night in the shower. In the secrecy of my bathroom. With water to wash it all down the drain. With the rumble of the shower to cover up my gagging. Right there. It was the start of the biggest battle of my life.

Bulimia slowly became a way of life, and I began to waste away. My friends started making comments, asking if I was okay. But my ex-husband told me he loved how tiny I was because he could throw me around on the dance floor, and his comments only confirmed what I pictured.

So I became a pro at covering it up, hiding in bathrooms with the sink and fan running, and using the handicapped bathrooms so I would be alone. I came up with excuses to leave so I could go purge. I chewed gum to cover up the taste, popping Tums after every time to ease the stomach acid, praying the dentist wouldn't out me again because of what the acid was doing to my teeth. No one knew. At least, no one ever told me at the time.

And so here we are. On the floor of the basement bathroom. Alone.

Defeated.
Disappointed.
Disgusted.
Shameful.

I was sure that one day, I would start coughing up blood, and my body would quit.

I wish I could tell you it all changed the day I picked myself up off the floor. It took six years, one drunken night of spilling my guts, and one very supportive boyfriend, my husband today, to break the power bulimia held over me. I decided I had had enough and quit cold turkey. If only the mental and emotional chains broke the same day as the physical ones did, but they didn't. They still haunt me some days.

I have gone through my ups and downs. I've loved my body and felt confident and strong. I've looked in the mirror and felt unashamed and unworthy. And somewhere in the middle were the days of apathy.

I am striving to write this chapter because I know it is still a struggle. I didn't know if I could do it because I've been struggling with loving my body lately. "That's okay. You may not be healed, but you are healing," she told me, a close friend and mentor, Melanie Wilson of She'll Rise.

The weight of the water

A few years later, I got baptized. I had chosen to be baptized as a teenager, but looking back, I was naive. It means so much more now. I volunteered to share my story during that service, opening up about my battle with bulimia. It was a plunge into the deep end, sharing my struggles with thousands.

The common perception of baptism is that it instantly transforms you, but the water doesn't physically alter who you are; it's simply symbolic. Going under signifies death to yourself, and emerging symbolizes a resurrection. Your anatomy hasn't changed, your DNA hasn't rearranged, and your thoughts have not been realigned. However, it marks a step forward.

In the moments before you come out of the water, you are struggling to breathe, feeling like you're drowning. Your only hope of survival is for someone to pull you up. When I was reflecting on this time in my life, this analogy of coming up out of the water resonated.

In the depths of my addiction and sickness, like that night on my bathroom floor, I was under that water, literally dying. Then, one day, I could finally come up for air—God pulled me up. I'm not magically fixed; the daily struggle persists. I'm still me, but I've taken that step forward to freedom.

I'm not healed, but I'm healing.

Jami KOLEV

Scan to connect with Jami

Jami is a daughter of the King, a wife to her best friend, a mother of three incredibly rambunctious beautiful sons, and a business person. She serves as the Marketing and Sales Operations Manager for a top real estate team in Southwest Florida, holds her Broker's license, and owns That Captivating Agent, creating marketing templates for real estate agents.

Originally from Denver, Colorado, she became a Southwest Florida girl three years ago, and you can find her on or in the water in her free time if she isn't at Walt Disney World with her family. Jami's life has been a wild ride, full of ups and downs. She has navigated through an eating disorder, weathered an early divorce, engaged in a tenacious adoption battle, confronted a life-threatening postpartum complication, survived the loss of her home to a hurricane, and grappled with grief, anxiety, and depression—each chapter of adversity having its purpose.

She loves to openly share her experiences with an unwavering belief that her path has uniquely equipped her to breathe life into the struggles of others. Through her story, Jami hopes to extend hope and strength to those facing similar challenges.

Chapter 12

Grounded not Braced

by Sarah Crawford

The response was quick and awful.

I had been practicing assertiveness, trying to express myself more confidently. I found an article that resonated with me with the intense and heated discussions surrounding the Presidential election. It seemed reasonable, presenting a different perspective, so I shared it on social media.

But when a close family member, whose opinion had mattered, ferociously attacked me on social media because the article was not in agreement with their political views; I was in shock, accused of terrible things, belittled, shamed and scorned. A person who should have protected me, along with others, attacked me. It devastated me. I shrank, hid, and allowed those loud, angry voices to dictate who I was.

A few people spoke up for me online, challenging the lies. Others called to check on me, reaching out with encouraging words and compassion. I was so raw that I clung to those quiet, healing interactions, attempting to let them drown out the louder, hurtful words.

But there was still doubt—doubt that I was safe. What if I upset those who were kind? Could I trust them? During one conversation, I expressed my desire to cancel an upcoming trip to visit family. I wanted to retreat. Some encouraged me to keep the planned trip and not to let others dictate my choices. I could take up space and belong.

When I was younger, I was told: "Not to wear my feelings out on a stick." In other words, don't be so sensitive, toughen up, and stuff down your emotions. When I visited the family I was braced for what the visit would bring. I tried to prepare for any unpleasantness; I piled on the armor and stuffed those feelings down.

I was ready.

Who am I listening to?

In the Garden of Eden, Adam and Eve lived in nakedness without shame. However, with the serpent's involvement, though they remained physically naked, they became filled with shame. They recoiled, withdrew, and sought to hide. When God approached to check on them, He asked, "Who told you that you were naked?"

Could God have been asking them, "Who are you listening to? Why are you ashamed now? I did not tell you to hide or withdraw. Do not listen to someone who could destroy you."

While I was still trying to brace myself, I read, "*As you, therefore, have received Christ Jesus the Lord, continue to live your lives in Him, rooted and built up in Him and established in the faith, just as you were taught, abounding in thanksgiving.*" **(Colossians 2: 6-7 NRSV)**.

Had I been listening to the wrong voices? What if I let being braced for the next attack keep me from remembering what I have been taught about who I truly am and Whose I truly am? What if being rooted in knowing who I am as a daughter of God means I do not have to be braced?

When I am braced, I allow the voices of others to shape how I see myself. WHAT WAS I THINKING? Why would I give other people that power over my sense of self? What I want is to be grounded in my knowledge of Christ. He says that I am loved and worthy and that it's okay that I am still learning because I am not complete without Him. I will be complete with Him.

How do we become grounded in Christ instead of bracing for the battering that comes from living in this world? We build our relationship with Him first, because as we come to know Him, we come to know who we are as well.

Establishing a sense of grounding requires trust. Trust involves openness—being unguarded, without armor, and allowing your feelings to surface instead of suppressing them—braced.

Instead, you will be open, to learn, listen, and be vulnerable.

The ugly prayer

I was 50 before I understood the need for the "ugly prayer," which just lays every emotion out before the Lord. There are things in my life I am not comfortable owning up to—thoughts, words, things I keep to myself. I have lived under a cloud of shame.

Not that I didn't think God knew all of my thoughts and deeds, but I chose not to face Him in those things. I went to Him with sorrow, questions, and requests, but I wasn't praying the ugly prayer. The prayer that says this is who I am, where I struggle; the sins I am afraid of are too much, and these are the things I am that contradict who you are asking me to be. These are the parts of me I view as ugly and don't want to face, much less accept.

When I started having those open, ugly prayers, I felt love. God already knew the ugliness. His Son is the one that has already overcome any ugliness. This was another step in believing not only in Christ's abilities but also in His promises. Based on **Revelations 21: 4**, He is the one to wipe away ALL tears, so there is no crying. He is why there will be no more sorrow, pain or death, essentially no ugliness.

It wasn't surprising that Christ has already accepted all of who I am. I was not keeping anything from Him. What did surprise me was that I accepted all of who I am. I am more comfortable being a work in progress. I continue to learn to accept that He is with me and that it is enough to keep progressing. As with all interactions with Christ, I healed. I do not have to be braced for what others think of me because I am grounded in the truth. God knows me, I am more confident in knowing myself, and THAT is who I am and should be listening to.

What is next?

The adversary wants you to believe that you are the sum of the parts that you view as ugly, shameful or unacceptable. That is where he wants you to stay. Hiding, afraid, and braced for the opinion of those who cannot see you. Who are you listening to? Are you adding to the voices telling you that you are not acceptable and never can be? Who are you listening to that may say your mistakes are too big for the price Christ has already paid? Is someone saying that because they do not understand your differences or disagree with you, hide, be ashamed, and change so they are happy with you? You can change who you are listening to if you hear these messages. It isn't always easy, but it becomes easier as you practice. Try these ideas:

Pray, and ask:

- Help me to learn how you see me.
- Help me to learn how you speak to me.
- Help me learn who you truly are.
- Help me see your divine hand in my life.

Read scriptures and,

- Look for examples of the characteristics of God.

- Look for how He works with those who are a work in progress.

- Look for answers in the scriptures. The stories do not have to mirror your story; being in the scriptures can allow you to be more prepared and receive what He is trying to teach you.

- Look for the broken, viewed as less, still learning and judged people that God uses to serve and bless His other children.

The truth uncovered

I would never tell someone I love to be sure and listen to the voices of judgment and shame. I would never tell one of my daughters to pay attention and believe anyone spreading rumors about them, especially if it is all lies or even if there are bits of twisted truth. I would do everything in my power to protect my four-year-old granddaughter—who is bright, happy, and sure of her ability to work hard, to learn and not give up—from listening to anyone who would mock her confidence and pick apart her efforts.

If I could do that for the people I love, why am I not doing that for myself? If you stand up for the people in your life, do you stand up for yourself? Will you root yourself in the truth of who you are as a daughter of God? Will you ground yourself in love, compassion and acceptance from God and what He expects us to have for ourselves?

Individuals who employ their voices to criticize and harm others with judgment and cruelty are often guarded or braced themselves. Often, these individuals grapple with their own insecurities, projecting their pain onto others. Embracing the truth of your identity and acknowledging your connection to a higher purpose enables you to recognize your inherent value.

When you stand firmly in this truth, the authentic self shines brightly, setting an example for others. The light emanating from women rooted in Christ and living authentically is more impactful than you may comprehend. Let's radiate that light and inspire positive change.

I choose to be grounded in Christ and who I truly am. I am a daughter of God, and so are you.

As an entrepreneur, Sarah Crawford has planned and decorated weddings, catered events, and sold ice cream in Alaska and at her current shop, "Spots Ice Cream, Crepes and Sauces" in Bokeelia, Florida.

Sarah will graduate with her Bachelor's in Marriage and Family Education in 2024. Sarah started The Connecting Joy Project to inspire joy by connecting the dots of faith, compassion and support for ourselves so we can do that for others.

Sarah loves to travel, spend time with family and friends, and learn new things, but she especially loves her husband of 31 years, her seven children, three sons-in-law and three grandchildren.

Chapter 13

Seeing My World in Color

by Nadia Parico Booth

Have you ever pondered the colors you perceive in the world around you? No, I hadn't either, until the day I awoke and discovered a vividness and vibrancy brighter than ever before. At that moment, the reality hit me that I had been navigating my life in gray tones, overshadowed by depression. Blues, reds, and greens existed but were devoid of life. My life itself seemed muted and lifeless—depression had stripped away more than I had realized.

The first time I noticed I had an issue with depression was during my sophomore year at college. I was battling sadness, lack of motivation, and feeling blah. What was wrong with me? Why couldn't I make myself happy? My mom suggested I talk to someone. I called and made an appointment at the school's wellness center. The counselor didn't impress me, and I quickly realized that I could manipulate our conversation and avoid sharing how I felt.

That was my only session with that counselor.

So, I set off to "handle" my depression on my own. I saw a therapist on and off for years, but I never connected enough with anyone to give a total effort. I went on and off medication, determined that I could control my depression. Well, that was so far from the truth.

Fast forward 23 years, and in August 2018 I found myself amid a mental breakdown. I had just returned from a weeklong vacation with my family and friends, but somehow I couldn't stop crying. I was very withdrawn during the vacation and couldn't figure out what was wrong with me. I stopped taking my antidepressants in March of that year because I had started CBD and felt terrific. But that was a mistake!

I made an appointment to talk with a therapist and to resume antidepressants. She recommended I go to the local mental health clinic so I could start their day program and get medication. I went, and after a quick intake, I started the program the next day.

I started my day in a small room with a dozen people, and they handed me a paper to fill out. This piece of paper was a daily check-in about what happened and how we felt the previous day. I just sat and cried; I couldn't fill it out. The counselor then went around the room, and everyone shared their responses. One girl in the back said, "We had a good night," and "We slept pretty well." The next thing I knew, they took her out of the room. That was when I thought, "This is not what I need!"

We took a break, and I ran to the front, grabbed my phone, and ran outside to call my husband. I just cried and said what I needed was one-on-one therapy. I wasn't comfortable talking in a group setting. He gave me some encouraging words. I returned to the program and asked if I could talk to someone, and they escorted me to a conference room.

A young woman came in, and I explained I needed to speak one-on-one to someone and resume my medication. She stated the program wasn't designed to be one-on-one and that the earliest I could get medication was about five days out. I didn't have five days. I decided to leave at that moment but couldn't get away that easily. I had to call my mom and put her on speaker so she would verify I would not kill myself. I never returned to the day program.

I called the original therapist and told her the day program was not what I needed. She said it would be two weeks before anyone could see me for medication and four weeks before she could see me. If I couldn't make it five days, I surely would not last for two weeks. In desperation to save my life, I started calling every mental health therapist's number in my area. I was so relieved when I found someone who could see me the next day. I resumed my medication, and it helped tremendously. I accepted that I would have to take antidepressants for the rest of my life.

The breakthrough

In 2019, my friend Melissa invited me to a women's event to meet a woman she believed could benefit me. Melanie Wilson, a coach specializing in guiding women toward wholeness and healing from issues like anxiety, depression, trauma, and addiction, spoke that day and immediately captured my interest. Her energy was infectious. Something about her drew me in and made me feel like I could share things with her. Might she be the person who could help me? Would she differ from the therapists in my past? Perhaps she will give me my life back?

I started this journey as my 17-year marriage was falling apart. My husband and I had become so disconnected that we were essentially roommates. I had been suffering from years of depression, anxiety, and incredibly low self-esteem, an overall feeling of failure in my marriage, as a mother, as a friend, and to myself for not completing everything I said I would do.

Our first meeting was in November 2019.

To say I was skeptical was an understatement. I had hope. How many times had I been in this position before? How many times had I told the therapists what they wanted to hear so I could avoid reality? She shared her personal story, and it was similar to mine. I felt like I was talking to a girlfriend, not a "therapist." If I was going to work on myself and heal, I had to be 100% honest and not hold back, no matter how badly I wanted to hide it.

As I sat in the booth at Panera Bread, I thought, "Oh my goodness, was there someone who was finally going to hear me?

Yes, Melanie heard me!

I cried because I felt exhausted and defeated and wanted to feel human again. Melanie was finally the therapist I had longed for!

She never allowed me to give her surface-level answers or make excuses. She validated how I felt and gave me the power to change and stop playing a victim. We dug in and went to what she refers to as seven layers deep. She would ask, "But why?" or "Explain more." With that, my first revelation came to light!

CONTROL.

Control was how I was managing life by trying to control every aspect. If I could control my interactions, I could hurt people before they hurt me or back away before they harm me.

I used to keep my husband at arm's length, constructing a protective barrier to shield myself from potential hurt. Man, the tears flowed at that ah-ha moment! That was a powerful awakening and set me on a path to understanding why I used control as a defense mechanism, ultimately driven by a fear of loneliness. The realization was the basis for changing my perspective and understanding that pain is a part of life, and it was up to me to handle it. Through extensive work and many tears I have rewired my brain and implemented the tools Melanie imparted, when facing situations I want to control.

This was also the time that Melanie brought me back to my faith. I was raised a Catholic and was a product of Catholic schooling my whole life, but I had lost my way with Catholicism and lost trust in the church. I found my relationship with God again and have been on a journey to strengthen that relationship ever since. I have listened to scripture, read the Bible, and listened to pastors.

I had a profound moment one night while I was sitting in bed crying because I felt so incredibly lost, and I was begging God to take the pain away. Anyone who has lost someone and the life they thought they were going to have because of divorce, understands that pain and how your heart feels like it's breaking. In abject misery I suddenly felt His hand on my shoulder and heard the words, "I have you, my child." The tears came harder. From that day forward, I placed my faith in God to help me through life's journey.

Having unearthed many discoveries about myself, and embraced newfound strategies, a beautiful moment arrived one day. It marked the shift when my world transformed into a vivid canvas. On that very day I observed my surroundings; the colors emerged brighter, warmer, and clearer. Inhaling deeply, I knew I would be all right. The battle with depression was mine to win, and joy was destined to fill my life. While the struggle persists daily, I now possess both choice and the necessary tools.

Is it easier said than done? Absolutely. But is it impossible? No! With the love and strength the Lord gives me daily, I controlled depression instead of letting it control me. Every day, I thank God for His blessings and for sending Melanie into my life. Without her, I don't know if I would be here today to share my story.

If you've ever felt trapped in the gray tones of depression, remember that you're not alone. Change is possible, even in the darkest moments. Take a moment to reflect. Are there areas where you feel stuck or enveloped in grayness? Don't be afraid to seek help from friends, family, or professionals. Embrace the idea that change is a journey, and you have the power to bring color into your life. Reach out, share your struggles, and be open to discovering the vibrant hues that exist beyond the shadows.

Nadia is a Registered Nurse residing in Delaware, and holds a bachelor's degree in Education. Perfectly Placed. Be Where Your Feet Are is her first published piece but she would love to write mystery/romance novels.

She has worked with Melanie for four years and has first-hand experience in changing one's perspective and living life to the fullest.

She is a single mom to two college-aged boys who are her world. In her free time, she likes to read, listen to music, put her toes in the sand, and hang out with her family. She desires to travel more and spend longer time at the beach.

Chapter 14

He Won't

by Melanie Wilson

"Teach me to do your will, for you are my God. May your gracious Spirit lead me forward on a firm footing."
—Psalms 143: 10 NLT

1:11, 2:40, 3:12...

These times flashed in bright red digits on the small alarm clock on my husband's nightstand.

It was impossible for me to sleep without the ability to quickly check the time.

Needing a clock nearby became a weird fetish, much like a security blanket in my younger years, and it had to be a digital version with glowing and obnoxious numbers.

Bizarre as it seems, I could not fall asleep or stay asleep if I could not wake up and glance at that clock. It was as though it gave me this sense of grounding, a knowing that allowed my mind to find peace. Peculiarly, it provided comfort and certainty—there was always a way of telling time within an eyeshot distance of my head on the pillow, even now.

As I lay awake in bed, the neon lighting became a fixation. Thoughts raced through my mind like a car on a circled track, so fast that I could not unscramble any of them. Anxiety took over. It felt like something from a science fiction movie where my body was perfectly still, unable to move, and darkness consumed me.

It would start at my feet and gradually creep up through my legs, stomach, and chest until my breath grew labored. Checking the clock over and over, this sensation of impending doom lingered.

Sleeping escaped me. Rest was impossible. I observed the changing of time, second by second, minute by minute...

1:11

...He put a dream and vision in my heart so vivid that I could depict what I saw in a drawing inside my journal. The clarity and unwavering confidence that ran through my soul was exciting and terrifying because with this comes risk, sacrifice, and trust that would run deep—choosing to share this with a select few demonstrated my maturity in faith, discernment, and the desire to be obedient. The sisters who held space for this guided me with the wisdom: "Put it in your journal. Pray over it. Be a good steward with the message He gave you." To clarify, they were encouraging me to be patient. Patience was not always a strong point for me...

2:40

...At first, Restoration Ranch was the name that felt well suited to this vision. Reflecting, restoration was a common theme running through my life and relationship with Him, and who has never required restoration of some sort? In the pages of {un}SILENCED, a survival biography written and published in 2023, detailing and capturing my story. It was raw, real, and honest. I poured out my struggles, trauma, anxiety, and addiction to share what is now my testimony of healing and His glory. He restored me, my marriage, and my life. I had this gut feeling that restoration would be what this new dream He had for me would be, and it would be a gift I could share with many. Being patient and a good steward of this vision would require my conscious refusal of wanting to take matters into my own hands. It can quickly become an active battler of wanting to take control and trusting in God.

There was a messy, elementary sketch carefully placed in my journal and a few notes that were so crisp in my mind.

"No one can prevent God's plan from being carried out. May Your will be done. Full Circle." 6.16.22. Beneath the words, Restoration Ranch was "*He restores my soul*" **(Psalm 23: 3)**.

In chapter 12 of {un}SILENCED, I briefly discussed the most significant move for us was to Southwest Florida. However, {un}SILENCED was finished and out of my hands before God revealed the depth of what He was doing.

Everything felt aligned.

I felt perfectly placed.

This time will be easy because I am obedient, faithful, and staying near Him. A common misconception of being a "good" Christian is that we will avoid struggles and pain and easily flow through life unscathed. For a split second, I thought that way—quite the contrary. When we choose to follow Jesus, we quickly encounter opposition. It can drive us to partial obedience out of fear, which is still disobedience. Take heart in knowing that if you are encountering any of these things, it does not determine your score for being a "good" Christian. He never measures our worth in such ways, yet we do it to ourselves and others.

Set that mindset free. It isn't serving you well and never will.

Perfectly placed.

The depth of what this would come to mean needed to be in focus. Yet, a battle began within me as I wrestled with this beautiful vision: where I once was, who I was becoming, and how to follow His calling without looking as though I was cycling back into old habits and patterns.

Have you been in a similar battle? Maybe God put something vivid, life-like, and colorful in your heart, and an old version of you reappeared to whisper why it is impossible. This is an unavoidable conflict between spirit and flesh, mind and heart, our old self and who we are becoming. He is there in every detail, catching every falling tear, and hearing every cry. You are His child, and in this current circumstance, you are held. A precious sister is waiting for what is to come through you. Be obedient and know that giving up is not an option. This vision, dream or goal will not only change your life but can potentially change the lives of many.

I was once a runner. Not the type of runner you most likely thought, but one stuck in flight mode. Running was a coping mechanism that I depended on for years to outrun my anxiety, depression, trauma, and baggage. It worked until it didn't. I never allowed myself to be perfectly placed. To be where my feet are. It was too risky, and the fear was so intense that running was my best decision–or so I thought.

This time, though! It felt like I could be running towards something spectacular.

Freeing. Life-giving. Purpose-driven.

His calling required my obedience, and I wanted to embrace it and run with fervor and focus on getting to it. Psalm 143: 10 became my life verse. Choosing a life verse gives you substance and strength, allowing you to stay on track and continue in your lane. It can serve as armor to combat the threats, lies, and schemes of our flesh; to pull us away from who He is calling us to be, what He is asking of us, and our willingness to trust Him in the unknowing.

Perfectly placed.

What does this even mean? Perfection? No struggles? Quick? Content?

There were so many ways to interpret it, but it meant I was where He needed me to be: willing, eager, attentive, and embracing it for all it is. Perfectly placed became a representation that I was uncomfortable, but being held. It meant I was incredibly fearful but trusting. It meant I did not have all the answers, but I trusted. As things unfolded, I had to tap into these specific things to endure the struggles, testing, and friction accompanying growing and landing where He needed me to be. Much like my story has been conveyed over the years, each time leading me to newness with favor and anointing. This new dream would not be any different. Is there a meaning beginning to circulate through your mind? Are you feeling a nudge in your spirit or a tug in your heart? Sit with it and allow yourself to pour it out onto the pages of your journal. Give it life.

You feel like He's calling you deeper, but the battles are overwhelming. Has He forgotten you?

You feel like you are being obedient, but there are more questions than answers. Has He forgotten you?

You feel like you are aligning with who He says you are, but the fiery arrows keep coming. Has he forgotten you?

He won't.

He won't call you deep and leave you floundering.

He won't see your obedience and ignore your cries.

When we walk in alignment, the attacks of the enemy increase. He does not require things of us that He has not prepared us for.

He won't.

He won't put a dream and vision in your heart or speak a word that does not come to pass. I knew this. I knew this with every part of my being, like a mother who knows the cry of her infant in a room full of crying babies. I knew, but as the struggle began, I started to doubt and question. Did I hear Him wrong? Was it a cruel joke? Who am I to deserve what He said He was promising? I remember going into that kind of dark headspace before, but this time I also remembered all of the answered prayers, the fulfilled promises, and those glimmers of who He is every step of the way. He has never failed me yet, and He won't...

3:12

...Moving to South West Florida (SWFL) felt like a pipe dream. My husband and I wanted it, but was it feasible? Could it be a reality for us to live in the Sunshine State one day? God said, "Yes," but in His time, not ours. We learned this on our own, much like Abraham and Sarah in chapter twelve of Genesis. It was thirteen years since God's promise to them, but it came to fruition. His "yes" does not always mean right now. He may also answer with "no" or "not yet." But when we submit a request to God, we can know that He hears us as we trust Him with our prayers.

We searched for properties, put in offers, and diligently pursued the move. I knew it was not the right timing, but my husband was honed in like a sniper on his target, and convincing him to slow down was an almost impossible mission. It was His plan for us, but not yet, and I felt a sense of peace. I continued to pray for His will to be done and for assurance to continue down the path, not knowing the outcome.

There was simply too much keeping us securely attached to Delaware, and even if we successfully purchased property, the financial strain and additional responsibilities would have been overwhelming. In my limited thinking, I thought this would be too much to manage, but this concern eventually showed up in a battle due to this new vision He gave me and He provided. My husband, bless his heart, told me to pray because God listens to my prayers and not his. This is not true, nor did it change the type or frequency of my prayer, so I pressed in and on.

He won't.

My prayers were for His will to be done and for fruit to be born became tangible as the loose ends began closing out, one by one, and the attachment no longer lingered. In a random search on the internet for properties in SWFL, which up until that point I had yet to attempt once, I stumbled across a property, and everything fell in line quickly. Not long after, we were loaded up and moving to SWFL. This was not His final place for us, but a stepping stone or point of preparation for the launch we never could have anticipated. He was bringing us full circle.

We closed on Full Circle Ranch at the end of November 2022 but didn't move onto the farm until the end of May 2023. In the interim, we had to carry the weight of two properties, and frustration and fear quickly escalated as showing after showing occurred, but there were no offers. Ironically, this was my hesitation once before.

Those darn neon red numbers on the digital clock flashed as a glaring reminder that I could not sleep.

I cried out to Him.

I prayed to Him.

I worshiped Him.

I spent time with Him.

He has never let me down.

He won't.

Once again, things unfolded according to His plan and in His timing. Full Circle is now a place for others to experience restoration, just as Psalm 23: 3 promises, and I am inviting, sharing, gathering, and giving in all the ways that bring Him glory. He has restored my soul and brought me full circle. Here I am, perfectly placed and embracing where my feet are.

What I endured and experienced over the years is being put into practice in a way that far exceeds my expectations.

Full circle. I can see it now.

It is possible because of Him. Possible, but not easy. This is where we get tripped up. I still wrestle with this as well. But you see the actions I intentionally chose and where the path led. What are you intentionally choosing? If it's not easy, but you feel like it's what He's put on your heart, do you find yourself in that struggle of questioning and doubt? I get it. You are not alone. But He will not leave you or forsake you. He won't.

Take this gentle reminder with you, write it down, and say it out loud: God's love for you is truly unconditional and ever-present. Unlike the love we may experience daily, His love is not tethered to ups or downs, nor is it dependent upon the work you do or influenced by your circumstances.

What if you are not stuck but instead perfectly placed by Him? This is not a moment of asking "Why God," but "How God?" Be still, breathe, and focus on failing forward, faith forward, and eyes on Him. You are exactly where you are meant to be, so be where your feet are, and know "*this is the moment for which you have been created.*" **(Esther 4: 14)**

Conclusion

The compilation of stories within this book stands as a testament to the profound impact of women who courageously shared their journeys of faith, resilience, and redemption. Each narrative is a beacon of hope, illuminating the transformative power of God's love and grace. These women, whose contributions to this book are nothing short of a divine gift, have embraced vulnerability and authenticity; inviting readers to witness the triumphs and trials that have shaped their lives.

Their willingness to embrace their stories with honesty and openness reflects the light that dispels darkness, enabling others to find healing and restoration in their own lives. Through their experiences, we are reminded of the timeless wisdom found within the pages of the Bible, which serves as a guiding light in navigating life's challenges and triumphs.

Perfectly Placed reminds us of the profound truth that a loving and sovereign God perfectly places us. Just as these women allowed themselves to be instruments of His grace, we are also called to embrace our unique roles and experiences, trusting in His promise to make pathways through the wilderness and create rivers in the dry wasteland.

These stories serve as a powerful reminder that God is always at work, bringing about new beginnings and opportunities for growth. As we reflect, may we be inspired to embrace our stories with courage and conviction, knowing that God is doing something new in our lives?

And in Isaiah 43: 18-19, "*The old has passed away; behold, the new has come.*"

About the Author

Melanie Wilson
She'll Rise

God will use your pain for His purpose, but in the valleys where it feels dark, lonely, and hopeless, it is hard to imagine how any of it can be used for good. Melanie once lived in that valley, but God fulfilled His promises and met her in that darkness. In that darkness He taught her how to be brave.

She emerged on a mission to extend a hand to women who may be existing in that dark space to empower them to look up and Rise Up.

She'll Rise is Melanie's response to overcoming a myriad of challenges—anxiety, depression, trauma, sexual assault, an eating disorder, opioid addiction, and a failed suicide attempt. She has triumphed and now serves as a beacon of hope and healing for women enduring silent struggles.

In her 2023 debut bestselling book, *{un}Silenced. Suicide saved me. The gift of breaking free*, Melanie guides readers through the transformative journey from pain, anxiety, and trauma to the realms of joy, glory, and blessings. Melanie reassures us that God remains steadfast in fulfilling His commitment to all of us. Melanie also co-authored the bestselling 2023 book, *Good Speakers Gone Great*, a collection of public speakers sharing their speaking experiences.

Melanie Wilson is an international best-selling author, speaker, trauma-informed mental health coach, and founder of She'll Rise. Through her intensive 1:1 coaching program, in-person gatherings, annual retreats, masterminds, equine therapy, and book clubs, she provides a comprehensive approach to helping women demolish the strongholds that hold them back from becoming who God has called them to be.

Melanie, a mother of two adult women, lives in Florida with her husband and raises and cares for her horses at Full Circle Ranch. Melanie is an active volunteer and, in 2022, received the President's Volunteer Service Award, which she holds dear to her heart.

Acknowledgements

He continues to amaze me with His grace, beauty, power, and love. My spirit is postured for obedience because He is calling me deeper, deeper still. Daily, I praise Him for His goodness in my life and for fulfilling His promises. All glory and honor is His.

I've sat in quiet local coffee shops, sacred spaces, on random benches outdoors, and stood in the aisle of my barn. Each place represents time spent with Him, praying, meditating, and writing. Writing {un}SILENCED, Perfectly Placed, social media posts, emails, text messages, etc. I'm attentive and expectant—He will lay the messages on my heart, and I will respond with gladness to share these messages with you.

To my savior for the gift of breath in my lungs. In 2015, I tried to take my last breath, but Your plans were in motion. I will choose to live my life in a way that brings You glory, share the love You have shared with me, and remain steadfast on this mission to help other women find wholeness and healing as well.

To my husband, who has chosen me every single day for the last twenty-nine years of marriage. You provide a safe place for me to find rest and fill my emotional love tank. We have grown leaps and bounds, matured, and found the sweetest love within our marriage. I'm grateful for who you are and who you are becoming. You are my hero, my world, and the love of my life—second only to Jesus.

To my daughters, family, and dear friends. Your unwavering support, love, and encouragement make my days brighter, and on the days I'm struggling with the noise of the world, you steady and ground me to bring me back to a place of calm.

To the women who make up our She'll Rise community for tapping into your radical courage to become who God has called you to be. It is humbling to be a part of your journey and exhilarating to see you breaking free and flourishing.

To the women who said "YES!" to this co-author collective project God put on my heart. Your stories need to be shared, and you overcame the fears keeping you silenced by putting pen to paper. I stand in awe of your radical courage, and we will continue to celebrate you every single day. Thank you for allowing me to be the vessel God is using to turn your story into a testimony that will bring God to life in the lives of the women who experience your victories.

To Richard Tardiff, my editor. Once again, you have come through to guide me and our co-authors through this process with grace. You held space for our voices and stories and "Richardized" them to flow so beautifully to have the impact God intended them to have.

To my publishing team, Oxygen. You provide the necessary nudge to take this project from a dream to a finished product that can be held in the hands of many. I had great confidence in you because of our {un}SILENCED journey, and you came through once again for Perfectly Placed.

Praise for

{un}SILENCED: Suicide saved me: The Gift of Breaking Free

"Melanie's story and journey of healing and growth from it is truly inspiring! I was able to relate so much to the content that it felt like she was speaking directly to me in her writing. It gives a lot of hope to healing and growing from trauma and anxiety. I also purchased the workbook that goes along with it and was able to dig in. I am also personally a part of Melanie's coaching program and it has absolutely changed my life. Without Melanie's story, we wouldn't have all of the benefits of her beautiful words. This one is definitely a MUST READ!!!"

— Chrysta MacBlain

"*I have just finished reading your book. WOW! Thank you for sharing your story. I related to so much of it. Especially the parts about your childhood and the relationship with your husband and your father. I knew parts of your story but never at this level and I'm just so incredibly proud to know you! I didn't realize when we met in June of 2019 you were about four years out from the attempted suicide. I never would have guessed that because of how much God did in your life and how he gave you the strength to coach women like myself. Now here I am four years out from meeting you and I'm living an entirely different life and, finally, can say I'm genuinely happy. You know that day we sat in Panera Bread, I didn't think I'd ever get to this point. But you did and God was in that moment. Because of your book club, you were able to impact Dawn, who shared a Facebook post that I saw. That was God truly. I will never be able to express how much you have changed my life. You were the one decision that changed the trajectory of my life. Forever grateful.*" — Christina Summa

"*As women, we have somehow learned to hide our real emotions until they rear their ugly heads through depression, anxiety, and withdrawal, among other things. Melanie shares her story in a very real and transparent way while giving glory to God who never left her side as she waded through the motions of "living." She owns her part in the damage that was done to her family in the wake of mental illness and anxiety. This book is such a good read and offers the hope that is needed along with thought-provoking questions at each chapter's end. You will be glad you purchased this and read it! Thank you Melanie for sharing so openly."* — L. Wasland

"*This book is a compelling story about the author's transformational journey from living with crippling anxiety, depression, and PTSD to a life of freedom through her surrender to Jesus, and the power he has to move in our lives when we let him.*

The author transparently describes her experiences, thoughts, emotions, and very personal battles with a humility that's displayed through her very raw vulnerability.

Her story is written in a way that is relatable to the down and dirty of anyone who has battled mental health issues with powerful ways to describe its impact on us and the ones we love. One chapter in particular hit me personally when she talked about, "collateral damage." These are the words she uses to describe the detrimental impact our unhealed traumas have on those closest to us.

Melanie challenges and encourages the reader to dig in and do the work while offering the hope we have in Jesus, to deliver us and transform us to be all we are created to be for God's purpose in our lives. Her passion and desire for others to experience this freedom and transformation through Jesus is displayed by the sensitive content she uses to reach the reader."
— Angela Holtswarth

"*Honestly written, vulnerable, and valuable. Melanie Wilson conveys her story through a beautifully vulnerable lens, highlighting her experiences, struggles, growth, and triumph. I found the book to be relatable and relevant and found the end-of-chapter guided reflections to be engaging and eye-opening. Highly recommend.*" — Thais Wood

To order **{un}SILENCED**

Made in the USA
Coppell, TX
28 March 2024

30659614R00085